LEGENDS OF WARFARE

NAVAL

USS Missouri (BB-63)

America's Last Battleship

DAVID DOYLE

Schiffer Publishing Ltd

4880 Lower Valley Road • Atglen, PA 19310

Other Schiffer Books by the Author:
USS Iowa (BB-61) (978-0-7643-5417-5)
USS Yorktown (CV-5) (978-0-7643-5288-1)
Grumman F4F Wildcat (978-0-7643-5433-5)

Designed by Justin Watkinson
Type set in Impact/Minion Pro/Univers LT Std

All photos are from the collections of the US National Archives and Records Administration unless otherwise noted.

ISBN: 978-0-7643-5562-2
Printed in China

Published by Schiffer Publishing, Ltd.
4880 Lower Valley Road
Atglen, PA 19310
Phone: (610) 593-1777; Fax: (610) 593-2002
E-mail: Info@schifferbooks.com
www.schifferbooks.com

For our complete selection of fine books on this and related subjects, please visit our website at www.schifferbooks.com. You may also write for a free catalog.

Schiffer Publishing's titles are available at special discounts for bulk purchases for sales promotions or premiums. Special editions, including personalized covers, corporate imprints, and excerpts, can be created in large quantities for special needs. For more information, contact the publisher.

We are always looking for people to write books on new and related subjects. If you have an idea for a book, please contact us at proposals@schifferbooks.com.

Acknowledgments

This book would not have been possible without the gracious help of many individuals and institutions. Among my many friends who contributed invaluable help in completing this book are Tom Kailbourn, Scott Taylor, Dana Bell, Tracy White, Rick Davis, Roger Torgeson, Sean Hert, and James Noblin. Their generous and skillful assistance adds immensely to the quality of this volume. Additionally, the very professional and helpful staff at the National Archives and the Truman Library went out of their way to assist with the project. Finally, beyond having the help of such wonderful friends and colleagues, the Lord has blessed me with a wonderful wife, Denise, who has tirelessly scanned thousands of photos and documents for this and numerous other books. More importantly, she consistently provided encouragement when this project seemed stagnated by various obstacles, and is an ongoing source of joy.

Contents

Introduction

U.S.S. MISSOURI

OVER THIS SPOT
ON 2 SEPTEMBER 1945
THE INSTRUMENT
OF FORMAL SURRENDER
OF JAPAN TO THE ALLIED POWERS
WAS SIGNED
THUS BRINGING TO A CLOSE
THE SECOND WORLD WAR
———
THE SHIP AT THAT TIME
WAS AT ANCHOR
IN TOKYO BAY

LATITUDE 35° 21' 17" NORTH

LONGITUDE 139° 45' 36" EAST

Three battleships have been etched into the minds of most Americans—the *Maine*, the *Arizona*, and the *Missouri*. Two of these are remembered for tragedy; the third, for triumph. Today, visitors can walk the decks of only one of these. *Maine*, raised from her watery grave in Havana Harbor, was towed out to sea, the bodies of her crew were removed, and then she was scuttled. *Arizona* rests, as she has since the morning of December 7, 1941, on the bottom of Pearl Harbor, a tomb for over 1,100 US servicemen. The attack on Pearl Harbor, which led to the sinking of the *Arizona*, brought the United States into the then-two-year-old World War II.

Just a few yards from the gleaming white monument that serves as tombstone for the *Arizona* and her crew, the USS *Missouri* is tied up; upon her decks the surrender papers were signed that ended the global conflict that the United States had entered with the sinking of the *Arizona*.

Missouri, not yet two years old when the surrender was signed, would serve her nation in two more conflicts—Korea, and the first Gulf War—before being moored adjacent to her fallen comrade in arms in June 1998.

During this service, which was interrupted by a thirty-one-year period of decommissioning and layup, she was awarded eleven battle stars and numerous other decorations.

CHAPTER 1
Construction

USS *Missouri*, BB-63, was the third of six *Iowa*-class fast battleships authorized for construction by Congress. The *Iowa*-class ships were the final battleships built for the US Navy and represented the zenith of design for fast, heavily armed and armored combatants. The lead ship of the class, the *Iowa*, was authorized on May 17, 1938, with construction beginning on June 27, 1940, at Brooklyn Navy Yard. *Missouri* was laid down on January 6, 1941, on shipways number 1, adjacent to where *Iowa* was nearing her launching.

The keel-laying ceremony, normally an extremely festive event, was decidedly low-key, with the public notably not invited as a result of security concerns, since much of the world was already gripped in war. Those same pressures had led the keel to be laid three months earlier than originally planned, and also led the shipyard to work in three shifts, around the clock, to complete the hull and prepare the mighty vessel for launching.

Ultimately, only four of the six *Iowa*s would be completed—*Kentucky* and *Illinois* were never finished, with *Illinois* being scrapped on the ways in September 1958, when 22 percent complete. *Kentucky* was 72 percent complete when construction was suspended in 1947; the hull, nearing completion, was ultimately floated out of the drydock where she was being assembled in January 1950, to make room to repair the *Missouri* following the latter's grounding incident.

Wisconsin, BB-64, while numerically the last US battleship completed, was actually commissioned in April 1944, two months before *Missouri*—making *Missouri* the last US battleship completed. *Missouri* was decommissioned the final time on March 31, 1992, several months after her sister ships—and decades after any other battleship of any nation was in use, making her truly the last battleship.

The keel-laying ceremony, marking the official commencement of construction of the battleship *Missouri*, is underway at the New York Navy Yard on a chilly January 6, 1941. Presiding over the ceremony was RAdm. Clark Woodward, commandant of the navy yard, second from right, who is seen here driving the ceremonial first rivet in the keel. *Naval History and Heritage Command*

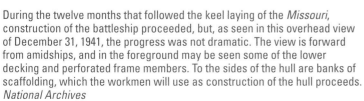

During the twelve months that followed the keel laying of the *Missouri*, construction of the battleship proceeded, but, as seen in this overhead view of December 31, 1941, the progress was not dramatic. The view is forward from amidships, and in the foreground may be seen some of the lower decking and perforated frame members. To the sides of the hull are banks of scaffolding, which the workmen will use as construction of the hull proceeds. *National Archives*

In a December 31, 1941, view from above amidships looking aft, transverse bulkheads are under construction. The hull would be built up gradually, with frame members being installed and shell plating, the outermost layer of the hull, being attached to the frames. *National Archives*

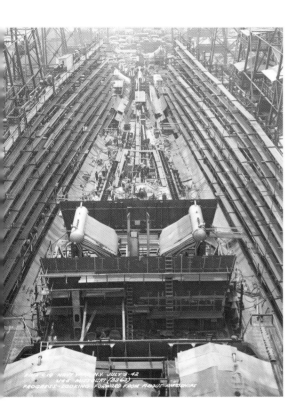
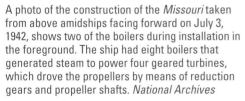

A photo of the construction of the *Missouri* taken from above amidships facing forward on July 3, 1942, shows two of the boilers during installation in the foreground. The ship had eight boilers that generated steam to power four geared turbines, which drove the propellers by means of reduction gears and propeller shafts. *National Archives*

A little under a month before the ship will be launched, the *Missouri* is viewed from abeam the conning tower (lower right, covered by a tarpaulin) facing aft on January 1, 1944. The conning tower was the heavily armored structure from which the ship was controlled during battle. Farther aft are elements of the superstructure under construction, beyond which are the aft smokestack and the foundation for the aft main-battery director. *National Archives*

Two days before the launching of the *Missouri*, the aft port area of the hull is viewed on January 27, 1944. The slatted structure around the port inboard propeller shaft is a poppet, one of several wooden structures designed to support the hull before and during the launching. Also in view are various shoring timbers, which afforded additional support to the hull before the launching. The propeller shaft emerges from the rear of the port skeg, which also served as a docking keel. Aft of the propeller shaft is the port rudder support. *National Archives*

A view of a point on the port side of the hull farther forward than the area depicted in the preceding photo shows the after end of the outboard cradle, part of the supporting structure for the hull on the building ways. Also in view is the after end of the port bilge keel, a low, finlike structure designed to reduce the roll of the ship. *National Archives*

The aft end of the port skeg and propeller shaft of the battleship *Missouri* are viewed from the side on January 28, 1944, the day before the ship's launching. The light-colored panels on the side of the rudder support are galvanic anodes: metal strips that protected the hull from corrosion. The black stripe along the hull is the boot topping: a paint-like substance applied to the hull between the high and low waterlines to prevent fouling and corrosion.
National Archives

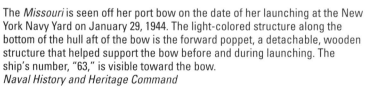

The *Missouri* is seen off her port bow on the date of her launching at the New York Navy Yard on January 29, 1944. The light-colored structure along the bottom of the hull aft of the bow is the forward poppet, a detachable, wooden structure that helped support the bow before and during launching. The ship's number, "63," is visible toward the bow.
Naval History and Heritage Command

The *Missouri*'s bow is viewed from the starboard side as she is being readied for launching on January 29, 1944. Suspended from the bow is a large bundle of drag chains, which will be released after launching to slow down the motion of the hull on the water. The anchors have been installed. Between the anchors is the bull nose, an opening through which a hawser could be fed through. Above the bow is the splinter shield for two 20 mm antiaircraft gun mounts. *Naval History and Heritage Command*

CHAPTER 2
Launching

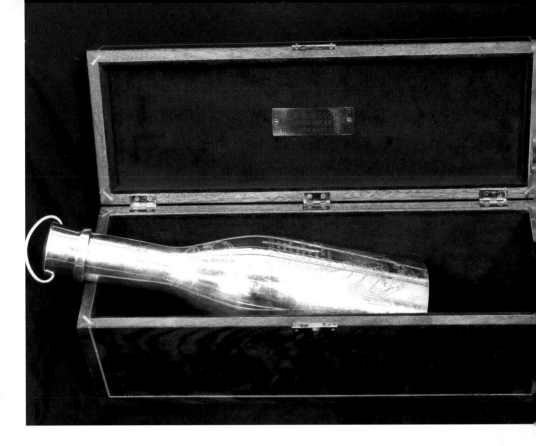

The container for the champagne for christening the *Missouri*, featuring an ornately engraved silver bottle cover and a wooden case with an engraved commemorative plate, is shown prior to the battleship's launching on January 29, 1944. *National Archives*

After months of labor, on January 29, 1944, *Missouri* was ready for launch. Unlike the keel laying, which had been done almost privately, the launching was a very public event. While indeed, in the intervening years, security concerns had shifted, some speculate that politics may have played a role in this, as they seemingly did with other details of the launching.

One of the milestone moments in the life of a warship is the launching, and the christening is arguably the pinnacle of the launching ceremony. The person who smashes the bottle of champagne on the bow and announces, "I christen thee . . ." is the ship's sponsor. In the case of battleships, which are named after states, the honor of selecting the sponsor is usually given to the governor, who often then names his wife or daughter for this duty.

In the case of *Missouri*, launched during the term of Democratic president Franklin D. Roosevelt, this honor did not go to Missouri's Republican governor Forrest Donnell. Rather, Secretary of the Navy Frank Knox invited Mary Margaret Truman for this honor; she was the daughter of Democratic senator Harry S. Truman, who was head of a committee investigating allegations of defense contract abuse and potential 1944 vice presidential candidate.

Regardless of the circumstances that led Margaret Truman to perform this duty, she did so with good nature and grace and began a relationship with the battleship that would far exceed that of most sponsors and "their" ships, spanning many decades.

At 1:05 p.m., exactly on the designated time and moments after her father's brief speech, she smashed the bottle of champagne on the bow, announcing, "I christen thee USS *Missouri*," showering both herself and adjacent Adm. Monroe Kelly with champagne— yet the hull stubbornly refused to move. Margaret playfully shoved on the great hull—and moments later it began to slide into the East River.

At the launching ceremony for the battleship *Missouri* on January 29, 1944, to the front of the bow is a press platform, supported by a tubular scaffolding frame. On the top level of the platform are about a dozen movie cameras on tripods. Between the bow and the press platform is a lower platform to accommodate VIPs and members of the christening party. *National Archives*

Moments before the launching of the *Missouri*, Miss Jane Lingo, maid of honor; Miss Margaret Truman, sponsor of the ship; and Senator Harry Truman of Missouri pose for their photograph. Miss Truman is holding the bottle of champagne that she will dash against the bow of the battleship to christen her. *National Archives*

Miss Margaret Truman is about to smash the ceremonial bottle of champagne to christen the *Missouri*. Also present are, left to right, Rear Adm. Monroe R. Kelly, Rear Adm. Sherman S. Kennedy, USN, and Senator Harry S. Truman. *National Archives*

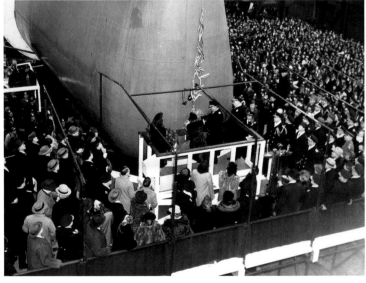

From left to right, Jane Lingo; Senator Harry S. Truman; Margaret Truman; Senator Truman's wife, Bess; and RAdm. Monroe Kelly, commandant of the New York Navy Yard, are on the christening platform moments before the launching of the battleship *Missouri*. During a speech at the launching, Senator Truman correctly predicted that one day this battleship would steam victoriously into Tokyo Bay. *US Navy, Courtesy of Harry S. Truman Library*

A cameraman caught the instant that Margaret Truman, sponsor of the battleship *Missouri*, broke the ceremonial champagne bottle on the bow, thus christening it. The extent to which the superstructure had been constructed upon launching is apparent. *US Navy, Courtesy of Harry S. Truman Library*

The ship having been christened, the restraints holding the *Missouri* on the building ways have been released, and she is sliding down the ways toward the waters of Wallabout Bay at the New York Navy Yard, January 29, 1944. Several men waving their hats are standing in the gun tub above the bow. *Naval History and Heritage Command*

The *Missouri* is viewed straight-on from the press platform as she slides down the ways during launching. A clear view is available of her bulbous bow, which was designed to affect the flow of water to reduce drag; this had the benefits of increased range, fuel efficiency, speed, and stability.
Naval History and Heritage Command

Most of the hull has entered the water, and the bow is about to reach the end of the building ways during launching on January 29, 1944. To the sides and above the building ways are the structures for the massive overhead cranes, used for delivering heavy components to the ship during construction. *Naval History and Heritage Command*

The bulbous bow of the *Missouri* has entered the water during her launching at the New York Navy Yard. Note anchors and launching drag chains. There is a clear view of the two bundles of drag chains suspended from the bow of the ship. *Naval History and Heritage Command*

The *Missouri* has come to rest in the middle of Wallabout Bay after her launching. It proved unnecessary to release the drag chains during the launching; they are visible, still bundled up, to the sides of the bow. A jack with forty-eight stars is flying from the forecastle. *National Archives*

OPPOSITE PAGE: As seen from the press platform at the New York Navy Yard on launching day, the *Missouri* has drifted far out into Wallabout Bay, with the Manhattan Bridge behind her. The drag chains are still suspended above the water. Tugboats are assembling to assist the battleship to her fitting-out dock, where construction of the ship will be completed. *US Navy, Courtesy of Harry S. Truman Library*

Tugboats are now maneuvering alongside the *Missouri* on January 29, 1944, to tow the ship to her fitting-out pier, where her construction work will be completed. It took a total of sixteen tugboats to move the massive hull to the pier. *National Archives*

CHAPTER 3
Fitting Out and Commissioning

When a warship is launched, it is far from complete, and *Missouri* was no exception. The thousands of tons of steel that Margaret Truman had christened and playfully shoved on was in essence only the basic structure of the formidable battleship to come. After launching, sixteen tugboats shoved the bulk of *Missouri*, herself thus far incapable of getting under way, to the fitting-out pier. There thousands of workmen continued to toil, erecting the superstructure and installing weapons and electronic equipment, lockers, machinery, mess equipment, and the millions of other components big and small that are necessary to transform a great, floating steel box into a functional warship.

As this work was going on at the navy yard, hundreds of other men were gathered at the naval training station at Newport, Rhode Island, where they were being honed into the crew needed to operate such a sophisticated vessel. While *Missouri*'s first commanding officer, Capt. William Callaghan, was with the ship in New York, her first executive officer, Cmdr. Jacob Cooper, was with the men in Rhode Island. After weeks of training, these men were later brought to the navy yard by train as well as the attack transport USS *Chilton*.

The *Missouri* was placed in commission on June 11, 1944, thereby officially bearing the USS—United States Ship—prefix (despite Margaret's launching exclamation) to *Missouri*. Among the dignitaries in attendance was the then-new Secretary of the Navy, James Forrestal.

Although the ceremony, which concluded at 3:22 p.m., placed the battleship fully in commission, there remained considerable work to be done. The remainder of June as well as early July was filled with provisioning the ship with parts and consumable stores and with dockside training for the crew. Finally, on July 10, *Missouri* moved across the harbor to Bayonne for drydocking and the cleaning of the hull, as well as final detail work. From there she went to Gravesend Bay, taking on ammunition from the Navy-operated Ft. Lafayette Naval Magazine. She was then ready to put to sea for trials and additional training of her crew.

In this undated photograph taken in or around March 1944, the *Missouri* is apparently undergoing fitting-out while moored at Berths 12 and 13 alongside Pier G at the New York Navy Yard. She is the dark-colored, large ship on the upper of three forked piers below the center of the photo. Alongside the ship, and partially obscuring the superstructure, is the massive hammerhead crane. *Naval History and Heritage Command*

With work on the ship substantially completed, on June 11, 1944, the *Missouri* was commissioned: a ceremony in which the ship was placed on active duty in the US Navy. At that time, the title "USS" (United States Ship) was officially placed before the ship's name. Additionally, the ship bore the designation BB-63, indicating it was the sixty-third battleship to be authorized for US Navy service. Here, the commissioning ceremonies are underway on the fantail of USS *Missouri* at the New York Navy Yard. The view is from atop turret 3, with its three 16-inch/50-caliber guns trained aft. *National Archives*

Naval officers and several Marines stand atop turret 3 during USS *Missouri*'s commissioning ceremony on June 11, 1944. On the deck below, in the foreground, are numerous civilian attendees, while farther back are the officers and sailors of the ship's commissioning crew, which was the original crew of the ship at the time it entered active service. *National Archives*

Members of the crew of USS *Missouri* and other attendees salute the colors as the battleship is commissioned on June 11, 1944. The view is from the after deck, with turret 3 in the foreground. The twin 5-inch/38-caliber gun mounts are set at maximum elevation for the event. As part of the ship's Measure 32, Design 22D, camouflage scheme, each 16-inch gun barrel is painted in Ocean Gray (5-O) on the top half and Light Gray (5-L) on the lower half. *Naval History and Heritage Command*

In a photograph of USS *Missouri* on the day of her commissioning, the 350-ton hammerhead crane on Pier G looms over the battleship. An excellent overview of the Measure 32, Design 22D camouflage on the starboard side of the *Missouri*'s hull and on much of that side of the superstructure is presented. The hull below the waterline remained to receive a new coat of paint when it went into dry dock the following month. When commissioned, the *Missouri* was equipped with the new SK-2 air-search radar; its antenna is the large, dish-shaped antenna on the foretop. The *Missouri* was the only *Iowa*-class battleship to be built with the SK-2: the other three ships of the class had the SK air-search radar, with its "bedspring" antenna, when built. *National Archives*

Following her commissioning, USS *Missouri* underwent a shakedown period from July to September 1944, during which time the ship was subjected to trials in the Atlantic Ocean to determine her performance capabilities and to remedy any problems that were detected. Here, members of the *Missouri*'s crew are loading the ship with case after case of Lucky Strike cigarettes, using gangways to the starboard side of turrets one and two. All three colors of Measure 32, Design 22D are visible on the gunhouse of turret 2: Dull Black (BK), Ocean Gray (5-O), and Light Gray (5-L). *Naval History and Heritage Command*

Crew members of the *Missouri* are loading bags of onions onto the ship in preparation for a shakedown cruise around August 1944. Loading massive amounts of supplies, from ammunition and fuel to foodstuffs and everyday convenience items, was a key part of the preparation for any voyage. *National Archives*

USS *Missouri* spent a brief period in drydock at Bayonne, New Jersey, in late July 1944. Here, the ship is viewed off the bow on July 23, with the bulbous bow and elements of the three-color camouflage scheme in view. *National Archives*

The bow and the forecastle of the *Missouri* are viewed from the port side in the drydock at Bayonne on July 23, 1944. At the top is the splinter shield for two 20 mm antiaircraft guns. Details of the port anchor also are visible. *National Archives*

The starboard side of the hull of the *Missouri* is viewed facing forward from the drydock floor in Bayonne, New Jersey, on July 23, 1944. In the foreground is the aft end of the starboard bilge keel. *National Archives*

The starboard bilge keel is also the focus in this view of the hull of the *Missouri* looking aft, in the drydock at Bayonne. The big, wooden keel blocks that supported the hull during drydocking are visible below the ship's keel. It was essential to arrange the keel blocks in advance so that the structural frame of the hull rested on them, to prevent damage to the hull. *National Archives*

Discharge water is spewing over the port outboard propeller shaft and support strut, in another photo taken in drydock at Bayonne, New Jersey, on July 23, 1944. The outboard propellers of the *Missouri* were four bladed, 18 feet 3 inches in diameter, while the two inboard propellers were five bladed, 17 feet in diameter. *National Archives*

Both rudders and all four propellers of the battleship *Missouri* are in view in this photo taken in the drydock at Bayonne. At the ship's required 33-knot speed, the engines drove the propellers at 202 revolutions per minute. *National Archives*

The outboard (left) and the inboard (right) propellers of the USS *Missouri* are viewed from the rear in drydock at Bayonne, New Jersey, on July 23, 1944. Keel blocks are arranged below the port skeg. To the right is the port rudder and support. *National Archives*

The stern of the *Missouri* is the subject of this photo of the ship in drydock at Bayonne on July 23, 1944. Details worthy of notice include the aircraft crane on the rear of the fantail, flanked by quad 40 mm antiaircraft gun mounts; the sponsons on the sides of the stern below the 40 mm gun mounts; and the ladder rungs just to the right of the center of the stern (eighteen vertical ones, and three arranged horizontally near the top of the boot topping). Faintly visible is the ship's name, embossed in large, raised, capital block letters across the stern at the level of the sixth ladder rung from the top. *National Archives*

This view from the afterdeck of the *Missouri* facing forward was taken while the ship was in drydock at Bayonne on July 23, 1944. Atop turret 3 is a splinter shield containing a quad 40 mm antiaircraft gun. The turret-shaped structure to the left of the quad gun barrels is the aft Mk.37 secondary-battery director, one of four such directors, used for acquiring and tracking targets for and controlling the fire of the ship's 5-inch/38-caliber guns. Between the top of the M37 director and the flag is the aft Mk.38 primary-battery director, which controlled the 16-inch/50-caliber guns. *National Archives*

USS *Missouri* is viewed from the port side in drydock at Bayonne on July 23, 1944. Turret 3 is to the right. Atop the aft Mk.37 director is a radar antenna; later, the Mk.22 "orange peel" antenna would be added to the right side of the main antenna on the Mk.37 directors, for better tracking of low-flying aircraft. Above and forward of the Mk.37 director, the aft Mk.38 main-battery director featured a 26.5-foot-base stereoscopic rangefinder and a director periscope. Atop the director was a Mk.8 radar antenna. Two SG surface-search radar antennas are visible atop the foremast and the mainmast. The big, dish-type SK-2 air-search radar is also on the foremast. *National Archives*

A view from the top of the gunhouse of turret 3 looking aft at Bayonne provides a close look at the blast bag of the left 16-inch/50-caliber gun. Also called bloomers or bucklers, the blast bags sealed the gaps between the gun tubes and the fronts of the gunhouses. Just aft of the turret is a gallery of nine 20 mm antiaircraft guns, protected on the sides and to the rear by a splinter shield. On each gun shield is marked the mount number of the gun; the closest gun on the left is 21, while the closest one on the right is 22. *National Archives*

The photographer stood atop twin 5-inch/38-caliber gun mount number 10, near the port aft corner of the superstructure, to take this photo facing aft, in drydock at Bayonne on July 23, 1944. At the center of the photo is quad 40 mm gun mount number 12 (gun mounts on the port side of a USN warship were given even numbers, fore to aft; mounts on the starboard side were assigned odd numbers), while the quad 40 mm gun mount on the main deck below has the number 20 painted on its shield. *National Archives*

Elements of the formidable secondary battery and antiaircraft battery of USS *Missouri* are on display in this view of the port side of the ship in drydock on July 23, 1944. Twin 5-inch/38-caliber gun mounts 2, 4, 6, and 8 are in view, along with various 40 mm and 20 mm antiaircraft gun mounts. Adjacent to the forward smokestack is the port Mk.37 director. In addition to controlling the 5-inch gun mounts, the Mk.37 directors also controlled the searchlights and the firing of star shells, for nighttime illumination of targets. To the front of the foremast, atop the forward fire-control tower, is the forward Mk.38 main-battery director. *National Archives*

Two quad 40 mm gun mounts are in the foreground in this view taken from the roof of 5-inch/38-caliber gun mount number 10. Below, on two separate levels, are eight 20 mm guns, with canvas covers for the guns and the upper parts of the pedestal mounts. *National Archives*

A 26-foot motor whaleboat was stored on davits on the main deck abeam each side of the superstructure. The one depicted here was on the port side, just forward of twin 5-inch/38-caliber gun mount number 8. Toward the upper right is the aft Mk.38 main-battery director. *National Archives*

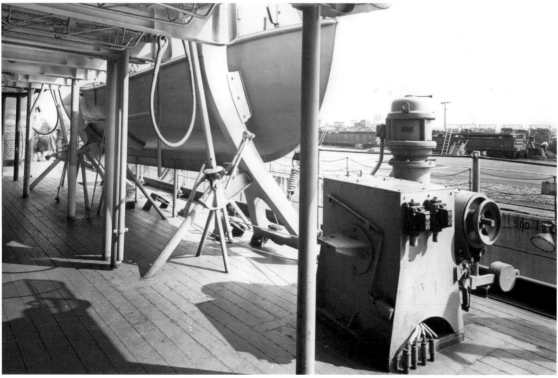

The port 26-foot motor whaleboat is seen from the front on its davits at Bayonne on July 28, 1944. The apparatus in the foreground is a boat winch. *National Archives*

In this view from the starboard rear corner of the level of the top of the pilothouse facing aft, in drydock at Bayonne, a signal-searchlight is to the left. The aft smokestack is in the background. On each side of the upper part of the smokestack is a platform for a searchlight. *National Archives*

In a view in the port side of the pilothouse facing aft, to the left is the side of the heavily armored conning tower, with a vision port equipped with a sliding block of ballistic glass in the foreground. A rack-and-pinion gear below the glass was used to raise and lower it. Inside this level of the conning tower was the ship's and the flag's conning station, and it included the steering wheel and engineering and navigating controls and equipment for controlling the movements of the ship during battle. In the background is a cushioned seat on a pedestal with a circular footrest. Nonslip-tread panels are on the floor. *National Archives*

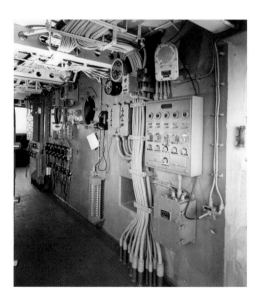

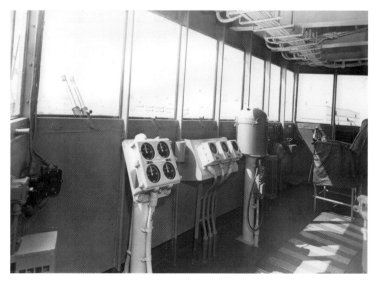

This is the pilothouse cross-passage, between the front of the charthouse (right) and the conning tower (out of view to the left), at Bayonne on July 23, 1944. In the foreground on the bulkhead are a loudspeaker, compass, chronograph, electrical boxes, and a multitude of cables. Farther away are two portholes with threaded studs around them, for dogging-down covers over the portholes. *National Archives*

The front of the pilothouse is observed from its forward port corner. This was on the 04 level, or four levels above the main deck, and also was referred to as the navigating bridge. It was glassed in for all-around visibility and protection from the elements. *National Archives*

On the 05 level, one level above the pilothouse, was an open bridge. This bridge is seen here from the top of the conning tower, at Bayonne on July 23, 1944. Various indicators are arrayed on the forward bulwark of the bridge. Below the bridge, the quad 40 mm antiaircraft gun mount emplaced atop turret 2 is visible.
National Archives

The photographer stood on the 20 mm antiaircraft gun platform above the forecastle of USS *Missouri* to snap this picture of the ship, the final image in the series of photographs taken while the battleship was in drydock at Bayonne, New Jersey, on July 23, 1944. In the foreground are the massive anchor chains. Farther aft are crates of supplies and numerous spools of rope. *National Archives*

After her time in drydock at Bayonne, USS *Missouri* was refloated and proceeded to anchorage in New York Harbor, where she is seen on July 30, 1944. A barge marked "Cleary Bros. No. 76" is moored alongside the battleship, and the ship's boats are moored astern. At this time, the *Missouri* was taking on ammunition. *National Archives*

Missouri is seen from the portside abeam turrets 1 and 2 in late July 1944, with a boarding ladder rigged alongside the ship. Details of the contours of the Measure 32, Design 22D, camouflage on this part of the ship are evident. All three colors are in view, from Dull Black (BK) to Ocean Gray (5-O) and Light Gray (5-L). Jutting from the upper-rear corners of the sides of the turret gunhouses are protective housings for the objectives of the rangefinders. Life rafts are stored on the side of the gunhouse of turret 2.
National Archives

A barge is moored alongside USS *Missouri* in this late July 1944 photo taken above her bow. Two quad 40 mm antiaircraft guns are positioned inside splinter shields on the foredeck to the front of turret 1. Just forward of those two mounts are two smaller splinter shields, each of which houses a single 20 mm antiaircraft gun. The box-shaped object on the roof of turret 2 is a splinter shield for a director for the quad 40 mm gun mount farther aft on the turret roof.
National Archives

The *Missouri* is viewed off her port stern while anchored in New York Harbor on July 30, 1944. The aircraft crane, used for hoisting scout planes from the water to the catapults, casts its shadow on the fantail. Flanking the crane are two quad 40 mm gun mounts in tub-type splinter shields.
National Archives

CHAPTER 4
Out to Sea

Missouri's first ocean-going voyage was a brief one, steaming from New York to Chesapeake Bay, where additional training and drills could be conducted in those protected waters, and also near the massive US Navy base at Norfolk, in the event of trouble.

During this time, the crew became finely honed, firing many rounds from each of the battleship's big guns and practicing procedures again and again so that they could be performed, almost by habit (much like breathing), in the event of emergency.

USS *Missouri* Data	
Builder	New York Navy Yard
Laid down	January 6, 1941
Launched	January 29, 1944
Commissioned	June 11, 1944
Decommissioned	February 26, 1955
Recommissioned	May 10, 1986
Decommissioned	March 31, 1992
Struck	January 12, 1995
Class	*Iowa*
Sponsor	Margaret Truman
Displacement, standard	45,000 tons
Displacement, full load 1945	57,540 tons
Displacement, full load 1988	57,500 tons
Length, waterline, full load	860 feet
Length, overall	887 feet, 3 inches
Beam, waterline, full load	108 feet, 2 inches
Beam, maximum	108 feet, 2 inches
Design draft	34 feet, 9¼ inches
Bunker fuel	8,624 tons (1945)
Endurance (design)	14,890 nautical miles @ 15 knots
Boilers	8 Babcock and Wilcox, 565 psi
Machinery	4 General Electric geared turbines, 212,000 total shaft horsepower
Speed	33 knots
Armor	12.2″ belt; 5″ on 50 lbs., armor deck; 60 lb. bomb deck; 11.2″ bulkheads; 17.3″ conning tower; 17.3″ barbettes; 17″ gunhouses.
Armament, June 1944	9 16″/50 in three triple turrets, 10 dual 5″/38 gun mounts; 20 quad 40 mm mounts; 49 20 mm single mounts.
Armament, April 1945	9 16″/50 in three triple turrets, 20 dual 5″/38 gun mounts; 20 quad 40 mm mounts; 49 20 mm single mounts; 8 20 mm twin mounts.
Armament, May 1986	9 16″/50 in three triple turrets, 6 dual 5″/38 gun mounts; 32 BGM-109 Tomahawk; 16 RGM-84 Harpoon; 4 20 mm CWIS.
Crew 1945	189 officers, 2,789 enlisted.
Crew 1988	65 officers, 1,445 enlisted.

The crew of USS *Missouri* is paraded on deck for morning roll call in this undated original color photograph taken during the ship's shakedown period. Tugs, including the *Camel* from Wood Towing Corp. in the foreground followed by four USN tugs and another Wood tugboat, are moving the battleship into a channel prior to getting underway. Painted on the roof of turret 2 is "40 mm GUN #1," with an arrow pointing toward that gun mount. *Naval History and Heritage Command*

USS *Missouri* is underway during her shakedown period, around August 1944. For security purposes, a censor has airbrushed over the big SK-2 air-search antenna and the smaller SG surface-search radar antennas at the tops of the masts. A Vought OS2U is positioned on the starboard catapult.
Naval History and Heritage Command

The *Missouri* is viewed off her starboard bow in a companion view to the preceding photo. The radar antennas atop the masts were similarly eliminated from this photo. The vertical chain cutting a wake in front of the bow is part of the paravane rigging, the lower end of it being secured to the front of the bulbous bow. Paravanes were in effect underwater gliders, which the ship towed with cables; the paravanes were designed either to cut the anchoring cables of submerged mines or detonate the mines. *National Archives*

USS *Missouri* displays the full range of her Measure 32, Design 22D, camouflage scheme on her starboard side in this photograph taken around August 1944. Not to be confused with black camouflage paint is the large shadow cast by the motor whaleboat on the side of the hull amidships. Here again, a military censor has eliminated the radars from the tops of the mainmast and the foremast. The censor also has airbrushed over the forward Mk.37 and Mk.38 directors and the radar antennas on the other directors. *National Archives*

The military censor's airbrush escaped this photo of USS *Missouri* steaming in a channel near New York City on August 3, 1944. Two Vought Kingfishers are on the catapults, and a third Kingfisher is faintly visible on the deck to the front of the starboard catapult. *National Archives*

USS *Missouri* is viewed from above and ahead of her bow during the shakedown period on September 27, 1944. Earlier that month, the ship had participated in maneuvers and shore-bombardment exercises in the Caribbean. At the time this photo was taken, the ship was bound back to New York from Norfolk, Virginia. *National Archives*

In this undated photo, most likely taken during the *Missouri*'s shakedown period, the three contrasting colors of the Measure 32, Design 22D, camouflage scheme and the asymmetrical layout of the camouflage patterns on the sides of the hull are clearly visible. *National Archives*

The *Missouri* was photographed in color off her starboard bow during her shakedown cruise in August 1944. During that month, the ship traveled from New York to Norfolk, Virginia; conducted exercises in Chesapeake Bay; and accompanied Task Unit 23.16.1 to Trinidad, in the Caribbean.
National Archives

Waves crash against the bow of the *Missouri* while conducting a high-speed trial run in or around August 1944. During the shakedown period, the ship was subjected to a series of such trials to establish the performance of the ship and to detect any problems with the ship's machinery.
Naval History and Heritage Command

The six 16-inch/50-caliber guns of the forward turrets of USS *Missouri* are unleashing a salvo during shakedown gunnery exercises in August 1944. All six of the 16-inch projectiles are faintly visible in the sky to the far right. *National Archives*

During shakedown gunnery trials in August 1944, the three 16-inch/50-caliber guns of turret 1 are firing a broadside. In the foreground are the anchor chains, and farther back are the wildcats: the capstan heads that acted to raise and lower the anchors. *National Archives*

Fire Controlman 1st Class E. M. Smith is opening the breech plug of one of USS *Missouri*'s 16-inch/50-caliber guns during gunnery trials in the shakedown period, in August 1944. Faintly visible toward the top of the rear face of the breech is the stamp of the US Naval Gun Factory, Washington Navy Yard. *Naval History and Heritage Command*

Several 5-inch/38-caliber guns of the *Missouri*'s secondary battery are firing during the night during the ship's shakedown period, in August 1944. These guns were designated to be dual-purpose, meaning they were able to serve as antiaircraft guns as well as fire at surface targets. *Naval History and Heritage Command*

One of USS *Missouri*'s big 36-inch searchlights is illuminated during nighttime. Although a crewman is standing by the unit, the searchlights typically were controlled by the Mk.37 directors. This searchlight was located on the level above the pilothouse. To the right is a Mk.27 radar, situated on the top of the conning tower; this radar was for ranging use. *National Archives*

Around August 1944, two members of the *Missouri*'s crew, Kenneth McNally and George Skiratko, are tending a 36-inch searchlight while it is illuminated. This was during the ship's shakedown period.
Naval History and Heritage Command

A number of officers are standing on the open bridge above the navigating bridge, or pilothouse, during the *Missouri*'s shakedown cruise, around August 1944. Four wipers for the glass windscreens of the navigating bridge are in view below the windscreens: three on the front and one on the side. To the lower right is the heavily armored conning tower, whose bottom is deep within the ship and which juts up through and above the navigating bridge. At the lower left is the rear of turret 2. *Naval History and Heritage Command*

As viewed from the top of turret 2 facing aft, the bridge watch was photographed in the starboard side of the navigating bridge during the *Missouri*'s shakedown period. The three men are, left to right, the ship's commanding officer (CO), Capt. William M. Callaghan; his talker, Yeoman 1st Class Arthur Colton; and the officer of the deck, Lt. Morris R. Eddy. Note sliding panels above the bridge windows and window wiper mechanisms below. *National Archives*

Cmdr. Hylan B. Lyon, the navigator of USS *Missouri* during the ship's summer 1944 shakedown, leans over his work while plotting a course in the charthouse. This compartment was on the navigating bridge level, aft of the conning tower. *National Archives*

Capt. William M. Callaghan, left, is in the navigating bridge with Lt. Morris R. Eddy and Yeoman 1st Class Arthur Colton, who is wearing earphones and a microphone for communicating the captain's orders to other parts of the ship. Callaghan is dressed in a khaki uniform, while Lt. Eddy is clad in wartime grays. Also note wiring overhead. *National Archives*

During gunnery exercises in August 1944, Cmdr. Jacob E. Cooper, left, the *Missouri*'s executive officer (XO), relays an order to his talker, Seaman 2nd Class Vincent Domino. They are standing in the open bridge of the primary conning station, midway up the forward fire control tower. The primary conning station was the nerve center for navigating and controlling the ship, except during battle. *National Archives*

A leadsman standing on a platform along the port side of the main deck is swinging his sounding line while measuring the depth of the channel as the *Missouri* enters a port in a mountainous area during her shakedown period, around August 1944. The man in the white t-shirt is a line handler assisting the leadsman; to the line handler's right is a talker. *National Archives*

A member of the *Missouri*'s crew reads a pamphlet during a break around August 1944. The pamphlet, titled *What about Girls?*, was an informational tome warning of the dangers of consorting with prostitutes; the author was Elliot Ness, the famed lawman and leader of the "Untouchables." Around the sailor are steel helmets, stored on the splinter shield of a quad 40 mm gun mount. *National Archives*

Some members of the crew of USS *Missouri* are assembled on the fantail while the ship is anchored in Hampton Roads, Virginia, during her shakedown period. On the shore in the background is the historic Chamberlin Hotel in Hampton. Three Vought Kingfishers are present, with practice-bomb dispensers shackled to the bomb racks under the wings. The director tubs for the two aft quad 40 mm antiaircraft gun tubs are marked in dark paint with the mount numbers 15 (starboard) and 16 (port). *National Archives*

Among the warships moored at the Norfolk Naval Base around August 1944 are USS *Missouri*, the largest ship, along the pier running across the center of the photo. On the opposite side of the same pier is the cruiser USS *Alaska* (CB-1), which operated alongside the *Missouri* during the summer of 1944. *National Archives*

A US Navy K-type blimp flies above USS *Missouri* during a visit to a port in the Caribbean in the summer of 1944. The ship visited Port of Spain in Trinidad in late August, and Culebra Island, Puerto Rico, in early September. *National Archives*

In a companion view to the preceding photo, the *Missouri* is seen from a perspective farther aft at the same harbor. The cruiser USS *Alaska* is at anchor in the left background. *National Archives*

The battleship *Missouri*, like other capital ships of the period, had extensive facilities for feeding the members of the crew, and feeding them well. Here, members of the mess crew are assembling dozens of lemon pies in the ship's bakery during her shakedown period in the summer of 1944. *National Archives*

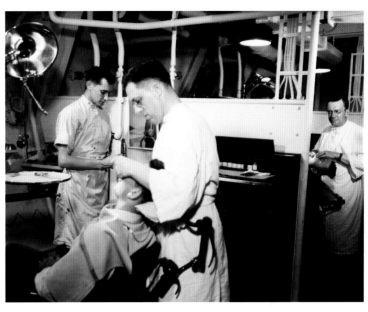

The *Missouri* had a full-service dental department. Here, dental officers Cmdr. Jessie B. Bancroft and Lt. George E. Wheeler are tending to patients in the ship's dental clinic around August 1944. *National Archives*

Machinist's Mates Reed Bankhead and Ralph Weiss are operating metal lathes in the *Missouri*'s machine shop around August 1944. The machine shop was instrumental in fabricating or modifying parts and facilitating repairs for the ship's structural and mechanical plant. *National Archives*

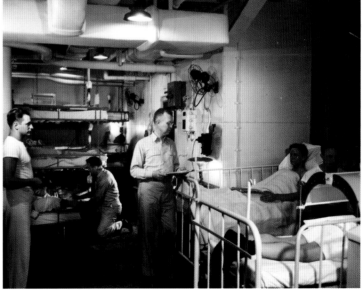

In the *Missouri*'s sick bay during her shakedown cruise, Cmdr. Louis E. Gilge, USN Medical Corps, makes his rounds while Pharmacist's Mate 2nd Class Frank Mancini stands by at left. The ship's medical department could handle cases from minor injuries to emergency surgery. *National Archives*

Lt. Rival Joe Hawkins, a chaplain on USS *Missouri*, leads a congregation of crewmen in prayer during a service on the ship's fantail at a port in the Caribbean during the battleship's shakedown period, around August 1944. To the right, a musician is playing a portable keyboard. In the right background is USS *Alaska*. *National Archives*

This summer 1944 view looking downward presents a striking contrast between colorful signal flags flying from the *Missouri*'s portside halyards and the gray twin 5-inch/38-caliber gun mounts and decks below. Painted neatly in white on top of the gun mount to the right is "MOUNT #2." *National Archives*

Band music was an important morale builder and entertainment feature on navy ships. Here, the *Missouri*'s band is performing a concert on the main deck during the ship's shakedown period. Note sailor wearing a red-and-white hat at left. *National Archives*

Gunner's Mate 2nd Class Charles J. Hansen is tending to a quad 40 mm gun mount during the battleship's shakedown period. His arms are intricately decorated with tattoos commemorating his service on USS *Vincennes* (CA-44) and his shipmates who were lost when she was sunk in the Battle of Savo Island in August 1942. *National Archives*

Crewmen of the *Missouri* are conducting an abandon-ship drill on the afterdeck around August 1944, during her shakedown period. Two Vought Kingfisher scout planes are on the catapults. In the right foreground, carrying an M1 rifle with bayonet affixed, is a member of the ship's Marine detachment. Note the variety of clothing and cap types and colors on the sailors. *National Archives*

A member of the catapult crew raises a green flag to signal the launching of a Kingfisher from the starboard catapult of the *Missouri* around August 1944. Two stacked pairs of life rafts are stored adjacent to the catapult. *National Archives*

Both of the crewmen of a Kingfisher assigned to USS *Missouri* are in their cockpits as the scout plane is being hoisted aboard the ship during the shakedown period. The *Missouri*'s scout planes were able to place observers high above the action during a bombardment so they could observe the effect of the ship's gunfire, so the fire-control personnel could correct the fire. *National Archives*

A Vought Kingfisher is coming alongside the stern of the *Missouri* during recovery, sometime in the summer of 1944. The observer, who sat in the rear cockpit and also served as the radioman and gunner, is standing on the wing, holding in his right hand a cable with a loop attached to the top of the rear bulkhead of the front cockpit. It will be his job to attach the hook on the hoist cable to the loop, so the aircraft crane can hoist the plane aboard. *National Archives*

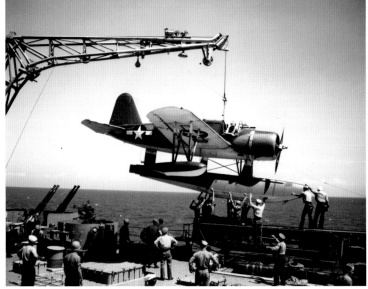

Crewmen of the *Missouri* steady one of the ship's Vought OS2U Kingfisher scout planes as the aircraft crane is lowering it onto the port catapult following a water landing alongside the battleship, during August 1944. Details of the construction of the upper part of the crane are available. *National Archives*

A Kingfisher is being hoisted aboard the *Missouri* following a landing. Before a scout plane landed, the ship steered in a wide arc, creating a smooth patch of water called a slick, for the plane to touch down on. This enabled a plane to land with relative ease, even during rough seas, as seen here. *National Archives*

Members of a film crew are standing by in the foreground (two motion picture cameras on tripods are present) while members of the catapult crew maneuver a Vought Kingfisher scout plane onto USS *Missouri*'s starboard catapult during the battleship's summer 1944 shakedown period. The Kingfisher is painted in the tricolor camouflage scheme of Sea Blue, Intermediate Blue, and White. *National Archives*

USS *Missouri* is viewed from head-on during a run from Panama to San Francisco, California, on November 22, 1944. Following her shakedown period the preceding summer, the *Missouri* had departed from the Atlantic with Task Group 27.7 and had proceeded to the Pacific via the Panama Canal. A close inspection of the photo reveals that the ship still wears her Measure 32, Design 22D, camouflage. Soon, a new camouflage scheme, Measure 22, would be applied to the ship while in port in California. The ship also still has her Vought Kingfisher scout planes. An escort carrier, either USS *Wake Island* (CVE-65) or USS *Shamrock Bay* (CVE-84), is in the background. *National Archives*

On November 10, 1944, *Missouri* left Norfolk en route to the Pacific. For this voyage she was joined by veteran battlewagons *Arkansas*, *Texas*, *Nevada*, and *New York*, and a host of other warships. *Missouri* transited the Panama Canal during November 18–19 then proceeded up the western coast of the continent bound for Hunters Point shipyard in San Francisco, arriving on November 28.

There she was fitted out with additional communications equipment, in anticipation of service as fleet flagship. At the same time her dazzle camouflage paint scheme, known as Measure 32, Design 22D, gave way to the somewhat more subdued Measure 22 scheme.

In mid-December, the Kingfisher scout planes were replaced with newer Curtiss SC-1 Seahawks. Though newer, faster, and better armed, the Seahawks lacked the fuel capacity of the Kingfishers, with a resulting decrease in endurance.

On December 18, *Missouri* left San Francisco bound for the navy base at Pearl Harbor; from there she would bring the war to Japan. Assigned to Task Force 58, *Missouri* served to bolster the antiaircraft defense of the Task Force, which first struck the Japanese main island of Honshu then moved on to Iwo Jima. Unlike the older battleships, *Missouri* did not participate in the preinvasion bombardment, instead remaining up to 60 miles offshore, ready to defend the aircraft carriers whose aircraft were pounding the island. In such duty on February 19, her gunners downed a twin-engine Japanese bomber, drawing the ship's first enemy blood.

On March 24, *Missouri* used her big guns in combat for the first time, not firing at enemy warships, the purpose for which she had been designed, but instead pounding Japanese positions on Okinawa. All told, 180 of *Missouri*'s 16-inch rounds rained down on the Japanese positions, the battleship firing at ranges from 17,500 to 20,000 yards.

Less than a month later, on April 11, the Japanese struck *Missouri* in the form of a kamikaze aircraft. Fortunately, the repelling fire of the battleship's gunners led the Japanese pilot to miss his mark, striking the hull side rather than the much more vulnerable superstructure. The bomb the aircraft was carrying failed to detonate, plunging instead harmlessly into the sea. The airplane's fuel started a minor fire on the deck, while the upper half of the pilot's body wrecked the basket for a floater net, and one of the Japanese airplane's machine guns was impaled on a 40 mm gun barrel on *Missouri*. Despite the protestations of some of the crew, *Missouri*'s commanding officer, Capt. Callaghan, ordered the Japanese pilot buried at sea with military honors.

The *Missouri* is silhouetted in the low sun while in the Pacific en route to San Francisco on November 27, 1944, the day before the battleship arrived in that port. After spending some time in California, she would sail with the same group of ships, redesignated Task Unit 12.7.1, to the Pacific, where the *Missouri* would make her debut in combat. *National Archives*

A second kamikaze hit *Missouri* on April 17, but this attack was even less effective than the first, with the enemy aircraft just clipping the top of *Missouri*'s fantail crane before crashing and exploding in the battleship's wake. Two *Missouri* crewmen were slightly injured by flying debris, which also tore the rubber gun bloomers on turret three.

After taking Adm. Halsey and his staff aboard on May 18, on May 27 she again shelled Okinawa. On July 15, at the urging of Halsey, Adm. John S. McCain, commander of Task Force 38, found some big-gun work for the battleship to do. That was the vicious bombardment of the steelworks at Muroran, on the northern Japanese island of Hokkaido. At ranges of 29,660 to 32,000 yards, a total of 297 16-inch rounds were let loose by *Missouri*. This was followed on July 17–18 by a similarly blistering shelling of Hitachi on the island of Honshu. With the war coming rapidly to a close, other than for a brief burst of 40 mm fire on August 9 these were the last rounds fired at the enemy by *Missouri* during World War II.

While undergoing improvements and conversion to a flagship at Hunters Point, San Francisco, California, in December 1944, the *Missouri*'s Kingfisher scout planes were replaced by the new Curtiss SC-1 Seahawk scout planes. Here, an SC-1 is being emplaced on the starboard catapult. This was a single-seater aircraft, with each of the three floats supported by a single, streamlined support pylon. The sling for attaching the crane hoist cable was to the front of the windscreen, whereas on the Kingfisher scout plane the sling was on the rear bulkhead of the front cockpit. *National Archives*

Huge waves crash over the foredeck of USS *Missouri* in the early spring of 1945 while the battleship is operating in support of the US invasion of Okinawa. While navigating turbulent waters in early April 1945, a sailor stationed on the forecastle was swept overboard.
National Archives

A photographer aboard the aircraft carrier USS *Intrepid* (CV-11) captured this view of Task Group 54.4 under attack by Japanese aircraft in early April 1945. The second ship in the middle distance, to the right of the center of the photo, is the *Missouri*. She and the destroyer to her front are filling the sky just above the ocean with flak in an effort to stem the Japanese attack. Accounts vary on the date and circumstances of this photo, some stating that it was taken on April 4, and others stating that it documents the moment of impact of a Japanese suicide plane on the starboard side of the ship on April 11. *National Archives*

The *Missouri* runs a gauntlet of fire during operations off Okinawa in early April 1945. A Japanese suicide plane has just crashed off the ship's bow, and there is evidence of a large explosion off or on her starboard side. It is unclear if this photo represents the crash of a kamikaze plane on the battleship on April 11. *National Archives*

The *Missouri* suffered a severe blow at 1443 hours on the afternoon of April 11, 1945, when a kamikaze pilot flying a Mitsubishi A6M "Zero" crashed into the starboard side of the ship. A photographer captured the scene a mere second or so before the plane (upper left) struck the ship at frame 169, approximately 3 feet below the main deck. Crewmen of the quad 40 mm gun mounts in the foreground are apparently going about their duties calmly as havoc is about to strike. *National Archives*

One minute after the kamikaze plane crashed into the *Missouri* on April 11, 1945, the ship is emerging from the cloud of black smoke that the explosion of the A6M created. Smoke is still boiling up amidships. The explosion was caused by the plane's gasoline. *National Archives*

A photographer on the *Missouri* documented the fire that broke out on the ship from gasoline from the kamikaze plane on April 11, 1945. Some smoke from the fire made its way below decks into the engineering spaces. *National Archives*

Crewmen of the *Missouri* are standing on a severed wing from the Japanese suicide plane. Later, the wing was cut up for souvenirs. *National Archives*

One of the machine guns from the Japanese Zero suicide plane was flung from the aircraft, and its barrel was impaled in the flash suppressor of one of *Missouri*'s 40 mm antiaircraft guns. *National Archives*

Crewmen are fighting a fire on the starboard deck of the *Missouri* after the strike of the kamikaze plane on April 11, 1945. To the right is twin 5-inch/38-caliber gun mount number 3. The small structure on the roof of the gun mount, to the extreme right, is a blast hood for the mount captain, to protect him from blasts from the firing of nearby guns while his head and upper body were exposed through his hatch on the floor. *National Archives*

On April 12, 1945, one day after the Japanese pilot crashed his plane into the starboard side of the *Missouri*, members of the crew of the battleship are preparing to bury his remains at sea. To the right of the saluting man to the left are the sailors who are bearing the remains. Research has revealed that the pilot was likely either Flight Petty Officer 2nd Class Kenkichi Ishii or Flight Petty Officer 2nd Class Setsuo Ishino, assigned to Kamikaze Special Attack Corps 5th Kemmu Squadron, based at Kanoya Air Base. *National Archives*

The Japanese kamikaze pilot from the April 11, 1945, attack on the *Missouri* was cut in half when the plane struck the ship. Here, what was collected of his remains are about to be interred at sea on the following day. *National Archives*

The burial party is about to commit the remains of the Japanese kamikaze pilot to the depths, aboard the *Missouri* on April 12, 1945. A Japanese rising-sun flag was draped over the corpse. *National Archives*

Members of the *Missouri's* honor guard fire a salute upon the interment at sea of the Japanese kamikaze aviator. Although some members of the crew resented rendering honors of war to an enemy suicide pilot, at the captain's insistence the ceremony was conducted in a respectful and honorable manner. *National Archives*

Adm. Halsey, center, receives a briefing aboard USS *Missouri*. He moved his flag to the *Missouri* on May 18, 1945, just before taking over as commander of the Third Fleet. The *Missouri* was ready for Halsey, having been fitted out as a fleet flagship while in San Francisco in December 1944. *Naval History and Heritage Command*

The *Missouri* proceeded to Guam in May 1945, where she became the flagship of Adm. William F. "Bull" Halsey Jr., commander of the Third Fleet. By now, the Measure 22 camouflage paint, which the ship had received during a visit to Long Beach, California, in January 1945, was heavily weathered. This is especially apparent on the Navy Blue (5-N) paint on the side of the hull below the lowest level of the main deck. *National Archives*

The 16-inch/50-caliber guns of USS *Missouri* are firing a practice broadside to the port side on July 7, 1945. At the time, the ship was steaming with Task Group 38.4 en route to the coast of Japan, where the ship would bombard the islands of Hokkaido and Honshu later that month. *National Archives*

USS *Missouri* (right) and her sister ship USS *Iowa* (BB-61) are steaming side by side en route to Japan around the end of the war in the Pacific in August 1945. This was during a high-line transfer of a group of armed sailors from the *Missouri* to the *Iowa*. Both ships are equipped with Curtiss SC-1 Seahawk scout planes. A close examination of the photo reveals differences in the radar equipment atop the foremasts. *Iowa* has the rectangular SK "bedspring" air-search antenna on her foremast, while *Missouri* has the dish-shaped SK-2 in the same position. *National Archives*

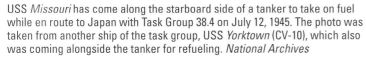

USS *Missouri* has come along the starboard side of a tanker to take on fuel while en route to Japan with Task Group 38.4 on July 12, 1945. The photo was taken from another ship of the task group, USS *Yorktown* (CV-10), which also was coming alongside the tanker for refueling. *National Archives*

There are various points of interest in this photo taken from above turret 3 of USS *Missouri* on July 14, 1945. In the foreground, there are canvas covers over the quad 40 mm guns on the roof of turret 3, and there also is a cover over the Mk.51 director, which controlled this quad 40 mm gun mount, to the front of that mount. Crewmen on the deck aft of the turret are napping, reading, or visiting. Pairs of life rafts are stowed under the catapults. A Curtiss SC-1 is parked on the deck, and another one is on the starboard catapult. *National Archives*

CHAPTER 6

Victory over Japan

The *Missouri* is at anchor in Sagami Wan (Sagami Bay) near the entrance to Tokyo Bay on August 30, 1945. In three days, the ship would be the focus of the world, as representatives of the Allied powers and Japan convened on its deck to sign the instrument of surrender. Visible above turret 1 is Mount Fuji. *National Archives*

In Harry Truman's autobiography, *Years of Decision*, he stated that once the Japanese had agreed to the terms of unconditional surrender, he was asked by the Joint Chiefs of Staff where he wanted this to take place. He opted for aboard ship in Tokyo Bay, close enough that the Japanese people could see that they had been defeated, yet isolated enough to protect the Allied leadership from last-minute fanatical attack. For a president from Missouri, having the ceremony aboard the battleship christened by his daughter was natural.

However, before the surrender ceremony there was a considerable amount of preparation to be done. While some of this had to do with the ceremony, more of it had to do with the reality of the actual surrender. Two hundred of *Missouri*'s men were transferred to *Iowa*, which served as a staging area for an occupation force that would go ashore, along with men from *Alabama*, *Indiana*, *Massachusetts*, and *Wisconsin* to secure former Japanese military installations. Notably, *Missouri*'s Marines did not take part in this; rather, they were retained aboard *Missouri* to provide security during the surrender ceremony itself.

On the day of the surrender, September 2, 1945, the ship's crew turned out to witness a precisely choreographed affair. The event began with a special prayer led by *Missouri*'s chaplain Roland Faulk, which, while remembering those who had perished in the conflict, admonished all to now proceed toward peace and rebuilding.

A number of dignitaries were aboard *Missouri* for the ceremony. In addition to Adm. Halsey, already aboard *Missouri*, there was Adm. Nimitz, General of the Army Douglas MacArthur, Gen. Joseph Stilwell, Gen. George Kenney, Gen. Richard Sutherland, Gen. Jonathan Wainwright, Gen. Sir Archibald Percival, Lt. Gen. Kuzma Derevyanko, Air Vice-Marshal Leonard M. Isitt, Lt. Adm. C. E. L. Helfrich, Général de Corps d'Armée Philippe Leclerc de Hauteclocque, Col. Lawrence Moore Cosgrave, Gen. Hsu Yung-chang, Adm. Sir Bruce Fraser, and Gen. Sir Thomas Blamey.

At 8:55 a.m., one of *Missouri*'s motor launches came alongside with the eleven-man Japanese surrender delegation. At 9:02 a.m., Gen. MacArthur gave a speech, which while outlining the terms of unconditional surrender also called for justice and rebuilding in the future. Following MacArthur's speech, Japanese foreign minister Mamoru Shigemitsu signed the instrument of surrender on behalf of the emperor and government of Japan, followed by Gen. Yoshijirō Umezu, who signed on behalf of the Japanese Imperial General Headquarters. Their signatures were followed by those of the Allied delegation, with MacArthur signing first as Allied supreme commander. At 9:22, the last signature was affixed, ending a ceremony broadcast by radio worldwide, and bringing to an end a war that had lasted for six years and cost millions of lives.

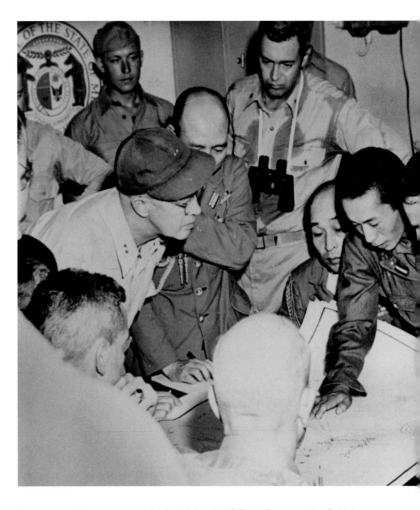

A series of high lines have been strung from the destroyer USS *Nicholas* (DD-449) to USS *Missouri* in Japanese waters on August 27, 1945. The purpose of the high lines was to transfer Japanese harbor pilots from the *Nicholas* to the *Missouri* by means of bosun's chairs. These pilots, several of whom are among the crowd on the main deck, would help the navigation department of the *Missouri* plot a safe course into Tokyo Bay.
National Archives

In advance of the entrance of Adm. Halsey's US Third Fleet and the British Pacific Fleet into Japanese waters, Japanese naval officers are reviewing charts of Sagami and Tokyo Bays with USN officers during a piloting conference with staff aboard USS *Missouri* on August 27, 1945. To the left, wearing a baseball cap, is RAdm. Robert B. Carney, Third Fleet chief of staff. Note the seal of the State of Missouri on the bulkhead to the upper left.
National Archives

A Japanese harbor pilot officer comes aboard USS *Missouri* with an armful of maritime charts on August 27, 1945. The charts and the knowledge of the pilot would help the ship navigate the waters to the surrender site in Tokyo Bay. *National Archives*

Officers and sailors in dress whites stand at attention, saluting, as Adm. Bruce Fraser, commander of the British Pacific Fleet, boards USS *Missouri* for the surrender ceremony in Tokyo Bay. The scene is on the starboard side of the ship, with the forecastle and its two 20 mm guns in the distance. *National Archives*

USS *Missouri* is anchored in Tokyo Bay on or around September 2, 1945, the date of the surrender ceremony marking the end of World War II. Curtiss SC-1 Seahawk scout planes are on the catapults. The ship exhibits a weather-beaten appearance. Sailors dressed in white are present along the rails. *National Archives*

The *Missouri* is viewed off her port bow in Tokyo Bay. The demarkation line between the Navy Blue (5-N) and the Haze Gray (5-H) of the ship's Measure 22 camouflage is readily visible on the hull. *National Archives*

In a photo likely taken on the same date as the preceding one, USS *Missouri* is viewed off her port stern. Several motor boats, including one flying a US flag, are moored to the rear of the ship. Large numbers of sailors dressed in whites are gathered on the decks. *National Archives*

The senior chaplain of USS *Missouri*, Cmdr. Roland Faulk, recited a prayer during the September 2, 1945, surrender ceremony. He is shown here on another occasion, conducting a service next to a 16-inch gun turret, with Seaman 2nd Class W. E. Britton playing an organ to the left. *National Archives*

VAdm. Charles A. Lockwood Jr., center background, boards USS *Missouri* in Tokyo Bay on September 2, 1945. He was the commander of Submarine Force Pacific in World War II, and following the war he wrote prolifically on USN and submarine history, such as the books *Sink 'em All* and *Hellcats of the Sea*. *National Archives*

Two of the principal architects of the victory in the Pacific, General of the Army Douglas MacArthur and Fleet Admiral Chester W. Nimitz Sr., walk side by side onto the 1st superstructure deck aboard USS *Missouri* on September 2, 1945. They are to the rear of Adm. Halsey's flag lieutenant, Cmdr. William Kitchell, the single officer striding along the deck. In the foreground is the table where the formal instrument of surrender will be signed. In the left foreground are the assembled representatives of the Allied powers. In the right background, photographers are standing on a temporary platform rigged for the occasion. *National Archives*

General of the Army Douglas MacArthur reads a prepared statement during the surrender ceremony on USS *Missouri*. Standing to his rear are assembled military representatives from the Allied powers. The seven officers in the first row behind MacArthur are, left to right, Adm. Sir Bruce Fraser, RN, United Kingdom; Lt. Gen. Kuzma Derevyanko, Soviet Union; Gen. Sir Thomas Blamey, Australia; Col. Lawrence Moore Cosgrave, Canada; Gen. Jacques LeClerc, France; Adm. Conrad E. L. Helfrich, Netherlands; and Air Vice Marshall Leonard M. Isitt, New Zealand. Note in the background the flag which flew from Commodore Matthew Perry's flagship USS *Susquehanna* when his fleet made the first visit by US naval ships to Tokyo bay in 1853. It was flown from the US Naval Academy in Annapolis to the *Missouri* for the surrender ceremony. *National Archives*

Facing MacArthur and the Allied representatives on the deck of the *Missouri* were the Japanese representatives. Standing in front are Foreign Minister Mamoru Shigemitsu (wearing top hat) and Gen. Yoshijirō Umezu, chief of the Army General Staff. Behind them are representatives of the government and the armed forces. *National Archives*

Gen. Yoshijirō Umezu, left, signs the instrument of surrender aboard USS *Missouri* on September 2, 1945. He was the chief of staff of the Imperial Japanese Army and was one of Emperor Hirohito's generals who opposed surrender. Hirohito personally ordered Umezu to sign the instrument of surrender. *National Archives*

Japanese Minister of Foreign Affairs Mamoru Shigemitsu, center, applies his signature to the instrument of surrender aboard USS *Missouri* while assembled Allied military officers, including Bull Halsey to the left of Shigemitsu, look on. Shigemitsu had a history as an opponent of the war. He later served as deputy prime minister of Japan. *National Archives*

First to sign the instrument of surrender for the Allied powers was Gen. Douglas MacArthur. Behind him to the far left is Lt. Gen. Jonathan Wainwright, US Army, who surrendered Bataan to the Japanese in 1942, next to whom is British Lt. Gen. Arthur E. Percival, who surrendered Singapore in 1942. *National Archives*

A photographer standing several levels up on the starboard side of the superstructure took this photograph during the surrender ceremony. Sailors look on as history is being made, while members of the Allied commands and the Japanese delegation are assembled around the table to the starboard side of turret 2, where the instrument of surrender was signed. *National Archives*

Following MacArthur's signing of the instrument of surrender, Fleet Admiral Chester Nimitz signs the document on behalf of the United States. Standing directly behind Nimitz are, left to right, General of the Army Douglas MacArthur, Adm. William F. Halsey, and RAdm. Forrest Sherman, USN. *National Archives*

In a display of US strategic-bombing forces, B-29 Superfortress bombers fly above the *Missouri* on the occasion of the Japanese surrender ceremony, September 2, 1945. At the center of the photo is the forward fire-control tower. To the lower right, a scoreboard is on the side of the navigating bridge, showing the ship's tally of Japanese targets. *National Archives*

US Navy carrier aircraft fly in formation over USS *Missouri* during the surrender ceremonies on September 2, 1945. *National Archives*

The Japanese delegation has departed from the site of the surrender ceremony (background) and is receiving honors on the main deck of the *Missouri*. The photographer was positioned on top of turret 1. Toward the upper left, alongside the 1st superstructure deck, is the temporary platform for photographers. *National Archives*

Adm. William F. Halsey, left, and VAdm. John S. McCain Sr., chief of staff of the Third Fleet and commander of that fleet's carrier force, Task Force 38, enjoy a moment together aboard the *Missouri* (BB-63) shortly after the conclusion of the surrender ceremonies, September 2, 1945. McCain was not well at the time, and he would die four days later.
Naval History and Heritage Command

CHAPTER 7
Homeward Bound

USS *Missouri* is just getting underway at Pearl Harbor on September 29, 1945, having been reassigned to the Atlantic. Three days after the surrender ceremony in Tokyo Bay, Halsey had transferred his flag to USS *South Dakota* (BB-57), and the *Missouri* departed on its long voyage back to the East Coast the following day. *National Archives*

At 5:02 in the morning on September 6, 1945, *Missouri* weighed anchor and left Tokyo Bay bound for Guam, where in addition to providing the crew a little R & R, several hundred combat veterans came aboard, to be returned to the states aboard the now-famous battleship. After a brief stop at Pearl Harbor, *Missouri* then headed for Norfolk by way of the Panama Canal. While at Norfolk, many of the crew, as well as the passengers, were discharged, and the famous bronze plaque, produced by the shipyard foundry, was installed on the 01 Veranda Deck, marking the spot where the surrender table had stood.

In October, *Missouri* moved to New York to take part in the largest Navy Day celebration yet, with a 7-mile-long column of warships. For the October 27 event, *Missouri* would have aboard President Truman and his daughter, ship's sponsor Margaret. After the festivities, which included numerous twenty-one-gun salutes, *Missouri* tied up at Pier 90 in New York Harbor and was open to visitors. Hordes of people came aboard, not only to see the historic ship but in some cases to take part of it with them or leave their mark on the battlewagon. Numerous small items were pilfered, and in some cases graffiti was left behind.

Following the postwar victory celebration, *Missouri* rejoined the fleet. However, due to her celebrity status, the mighty warship was frequently used to "show the flag," visiting allied nations and politically sensitive areas worldwide. During this time *Missouri* also served as a transport to bring President Truman and his family back from South America.

During the late 1940s, *Missouri* was used primarily as a training ship, especially for midshipmen cruises. Usually such service is uneventful, but in the case of *Missouri*, however, all too soon this would change.

Four weeks after the surrender ceremony, sailors are holystoning the area of the 1st superstructure deck of USS *Missouri*, where the ceremony had taken place. They are clutching the poles of the holystones in approved USN fashion. The purpose of the exercise was to remove the paint from the wooden deck. *National Archives*

This aerial view captures the *Missouri* as she is traversing the Panama Canal on her way back to the East Coast on October 13, 1945. A tugboat off the ship's starboard bow is helping to guide her to the Miraflores Locks in the background. Several of the *Missouri*'s Curtiss SC-1 scout planes are stored on the afterdeck with wings folded. *National Archives*

It is a tight fit, but USS *Missouri* is making its way through the Miraflores Locks on the Panama Canal on October 13, 1945. The traversing of the Panama Canal was always an object of interest to the crews of ships, and many members of *Missouri*'s crew are on the decks, enjoying the sights. *National Archives*

USS *Missouri* has just exited Miraflores Locks on the Panama Canal during her eastward journey, destination New York City, on October 13, 1945. In these photos from the Panama Canal, it is evident that most, if not all, of the Deck Blue (20-B) paint has been holystoned and washed from the wooden decks. *National Archives*

Crewmen of USS *Missouri* are being paraded at quarters in early October 1945 as the battleship proceeds toward New York City to participate in the Navy Day Fleet Review. At the bottom of the photo is the antenna of the Mk.12/22 radar atop the forward Mk.37 director. To the front of the antenna is the oval roof of the conning tower, on which are mounted four periscope heads and a Mk.27 fire-control radar antenna. *National Archives*

Sailors are departing from USS *Missouri* at Naval Operating Base Norfolk, Virginia, around October 18, 1945. Their next stop will be discharge centers, where they will be mustered out of the US Navy. In the background are, left to right, the *Missouri*'s aft smokestack, her aft fire-control tower and Mk.38 main-battery director, and the aft Mk.37 secondary-battery director. *National Archives*

Signalman 3rd Class Jose de la Torre Jr., left, applies fine touches to a mural being painted on the forward bulkhead of the wardroom of USS *Missouri* in preparation for public tours of the ship during Navy Day at New York City on October 27, 1945. The photo was taken around October 25. Also present are Signalman 2nd Class Gerald Parker and Lt. (junior grade) Reichart Muncie Jr. *National Archives*

Members of the crew of USS *Missouri* are manning the rails during Navy Day observances while the ship is anchored in the Hudson River off Manhattan on October 27, 1945. Moored alongside the battleship is the destroyer USS *Renshaw* (DD-499). For these observances, the names of the ships were painted in large, white block letters amidships on the hulls to help spectators identify the ships; *Renshaw*'s is visible here, but the destroyer is covering the name on *Missouri*'s hull. *National Archives*

The "MISSOURI" inscription in white paint on the side of the hull, installed for the 1945 Navy Day celebrations, is visible in this photo of the ship while anchored at New York in late October 1945. Two landing craft are moored alongside the ship below the "MISSOURI" markings. One year and nine months after her launching, the *Missouri* had returned to the place of her birth. *US Navy*

The battleship *Missouri* is observed off her port beam, showing details of the amidships area, at around the time of the Navy Day 1945 festivities in New York. The ship still had the dish-shaped SK-2 air-search radar antenna on her foretop, and she would retain that antenna until a 1948 refitting. *US Navy*

USS *Missouri* is viewed from a position farther forward on or around Navy Day 1945. The ship, particularly the hull, was heavily weathered and in need of repainting. The Navy Day celebration is an annual event, marking the birth of the US Navy, but the 1945 edition was a very special event, constituting in effect a celebration of the victory in World War II. *US Navy*

USS *Missouri* is viewed from the starboard side directly abeam the two smokestacks around the time of Navy Day 1945 at New York. This battleship was but one of the many US Navy ships anchored on the Hudson River for the event. *US Navy*

The day after Navy Day 1945, the *Missouri* left her anchorage in the Hudson River and repaired to Pier 90 on Manhattan's West Side, as seen here. A "WELCOME HOME" sign is painted on the upper part of the building. The ship remained docked there for one and a half weeks, during which time an estimated 750,000 visitors toured the ship. *US Navy*

Throngs of visitors are gathered on the starboard side of USS *Missouri* near quad 40 mm gun mount number 17 while the ship is docked in New York. Note the wedge-shaped covers over the automatic ammunition feed mechanisms atop the guns' receivers. *National Archives*

The *Missouri* is viewed off her port bow while docked at Pier 90 in Manhattan in 1945. Recently the ship had been repainted in Measure 21 camouflage, with Navy Blue (5-N) on all vertical surfaces and Deck Blue (20-B) on horizontal surfaces. Graffiti is present on the front of the splinter shield of the two 20 mm guns on the forecastle, including "Hoppy Kelly." The ship's number, "63," is painted on the side of the bow. *National Archives*

In early 1946, USS *Missouri* was dispatched to the Mediterranean on a combination goodwill voyage and display of military power, to demonstrate US resolve to prevent Soviet meddling in the area. The battleship also had another mission: to return the remains of the late Turkish ambassador to the United States, Mehmet Munir Ertegun, to his homeland. Here, the body of Ambassador Ertegun is about to be lowered, with full military honors, from the *Missouri* while anchored in the Bosphorous off Istanbul, Turkey. *National Archives*

During her voyage to the Mediterranean in 1946, USS *Missouri* is seen at the center of the photo at anchor in the Bosphorous off Istanbul in early April, with Dolmabahçe Mosque in the foreground. The destroyer USS *Power* (DD-839) is to the left, and the Turkish battlecruiser *Yavuz* (ex-Imperial German Navy SMS *Goeben*) is at the right. The ship had been repainted in the standard postwar US Navy camouflage scheme of Haze Gray (5-H) on all of the vertical surfaces and Deck Blue (20-B) on horizontal surfaces. *National Archives*

A Sikorsky HO3S helicopter has landed on the roof of turret 1 of USS *Missouri* during the spring of 1947. Helicopters were just becoming operational with the navy, and their full potential as transport and observation aircraft would become evident in coming years. Ultimately, the *Missouri* would be equipped with a helipad on the fantail. *National Archives*

USS *Missouri* visited Rio de Janeiro, Brazil, in the summer of 1947. President Harry S. Truman was visiting that country at the same time, and on September 2 he and President Eurica Gaspar Dutra of Brazil came aboard the battleship for a reception. Five days later, President Truman and his family boarded the *Missouri* for their return voyage to the United States.
US Navy, Courtesy of Harry S. Truman Library

President Truman was initiated as a "Trusty Shellback" in a Neptune Party when USS *Missouri* crossed the equator during its return voyage from Brazil to the United States on September 11, 1947. He was the first "Pollywog" to be summoned before the "Court of Neptune," which issued certificates to men of all ranks and stations as proof that he had crossed the equator. The president was spared the indignity of having to don outlandish dress, as most Pollywogs were obligated to do. *US Navy, Courtesy of Harry S. Truman Library*

During the return voyage of USS *Missouri* from Brazil in September 1947, Bess Truman (third from left) enjoys lunch with some members of the ship's crew. Other members of President Truman's party were also present for this meal. *US Navy, Courtesy of Harry S. Truman Library*

On the *Missouri* during the Neptune Party on her return voyage from Brazil, Pollywog Merriman Smith, a member of the press, has been tossed backward from a teetering chair into the Royal Tank, where sailors covered in grease are giving him a dunking. *US Navy, Courtesy of Harry S. Truman Library*

In the summer of 1948, USS *Missouri* was host to a midshipmen's cruise to the Mediterranean. In a midshipmen's cruise, members of the US Naval Academy received on-ship training in the practical matters of a warship. The ship is shown here during that cruise in the middle of the Atlantic Ocean, as hundreds of midshipmen and members of the crew take a swim. Several years before, new Mk.13 radar antennas had been installed atop the two Mk.38 main-battery directors, and a new, tripod mainmast had been installed on the rear of the aft smokestack. *Missouri* also had been refitted with a new SR-3 air-search radar antenna on the foremast and an SP height-finder antenna atop the mainmast. *National Archives*

During the 1948 midshipmen's cruise, on August 17, Boiler Tender 1st Class Hans Jacobs, kneeling to the left, demonstrates for two midshipmen how to light-off a boiler. The midshipmen are William B. Anderson Jr. and, holding the lighting torch, Charles A. Bivenour Jr. *National Archives*

Midshipmen and crewmen take the opportunity to sunbathe on the fantail of USS *Missouri* during the summer 1948 midshipmen's cruise. In the foreground are the wings of the two Curtiss SC-1 scout planes on the catapults. Stored on the deck farther forward is an array of the ship's boats. Even farther forward are turret 3, the aft fire-control tower, and the twin 5-inch/38-caliber gun mounts, with guns aimed skyward. *National Archives*

Midshipmen from the US Naval Academy at Annapolis, Maryland, chow down in a mess area on USS *Missouri* during their training cruise on September 13, 1948. Although the crew sometimes groused about the food, the mess staff took pride in feeding large numbers of men good, nourishing meals. *National Archives*

A Sikorski HO3S-1 helicopter comes down for a landing on the impromptu helipad on the roof of turret 1 aboard USS *Missouri* on September 13, 1948. This helicopter was USN Bureau Number (BuNo) 122527; Bureau Numbers are the Navy's serial numbers, and in this case it is painted in small figures on the boom. *National Archives*

USS *Missouri* was photographed from an aircraft during her return from Operation Frigid on November 20, 1948, with two aircraft carriers, USS *Philippine Sea* (CVA-47) and USS *Leyte* (CVA-32), in the distance. The 40 mm and 20 mm gun mounts had been removed from the main deck and the forecastle by now. *National Archives*

This aerial photograph of the *Missouri* was also taken on November 20, 1948, during her return from Operation Frigid. Two Curtiss SC-1 scout planes are on the catapults, bearing the numbers 4 and 12 on the fuselages and the tail code UC. The ship shows evidence of having been painted fairly recently. *National Archives*

USS *Missouri* steams alongside the hospital ship USS *Consolation* (AH-15) and the destroyer USS *Stormes* (DD-789) in the North Atlantic during Operation Frigid on November 13, 1948. This operation was a series of cold-weather maneuvers by the 2nd Task Fleet in the Greenland area in the first half of November 1948. *National Archives*

Two tugboats are assisting USS *Missouri* to maneuver next to a pier at Cristobal, Canal Zone, on April 30, 1949. The ship was in the area during a Naval Reserve training cruise. At this time, the aircraft crane and the two catapults on the fantail were still present, but they soon would be removed. Two quad 40 mm gun mounts are still located in the tubs on the fantail as well. Awnings are erected to the front and to the rear of the superstructure. *National Archives*

At the center of the photo, a TDD target drone is being launched from a catapult on the port side of USS *Missouri* during Atlantic Command maneuvers off Vieques, Puerto Rico, on March 11, 1949. To the left, standing atop turret 3, is the drone-control officer, holding the remote control. Produced in large numbers by the Radioplane Company, the piston-engined TDD (Target Drone Denny) provided the navy with an inexpensive aerial target for use in antiaircraft firing drills. *National Archives*

Between May and August 1949 the catapults were removed from the fantail of USS *Missouri*. With those fixtures deleted, there now was space for helicopters to land on and take off from the fantail. In this photo taken on August 8, 1949, Sikorsky HO3S-1, BuNo 123139, is parked crosswise on the fantail of the ship. The fuselage code UR-5 is visible on the aircraft. The view is from above turret 3. Note the collection of motorized boats stored aft of the turret. A boat number in the form of "Mo" followed by a numeral is on each side of the bow of each boat. *National Archives*

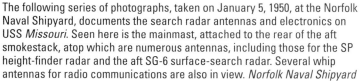

The following series of photographs, taken on January 5, 1950, at the Norfolk Naval Shipyard, documents the search radar antennas and electronics on USS *Missouri*. Seen here is the mainmast, attached to the rear of the aft smokestack, atop which are numerous antennas, including those for the SP height-finder radar and the aft SG-6 surface-search radar. Several whip antennas for radio communications are also in view. *Norfolk Naval Shipyard*

The overall arrangement of electronics and radio and radar antennas on the foremast of USS *Missouri* is portrayed in this photo taken from the port side of her forward superstructure at Norfolk on January 5, 1950. Note the dish-type Mk.25 radar antennas on the forward Mk.37 director (far left; the antenna is pointed upward) and on the port Mk.37 director (right of center). These radars were installed during a 1948 modernization and were an improvement over the old Mk.12/22 radar. *Norfolk Naval Shipyard*

The antennas on top of the foremast are viewed from the port side in this photo taken from an elevated position to the port side of the foretop. To the lower left is the antenna for the SR-3 air-search radar, which would prove to be problem plagued in service. The dish-type antenna on the foretop to the right is the forward SG-6 surface-search radar. On the topmast aft of the SG-6 antenna are RDZ and TDZ UHF-radio antennas. *Norfolk Naval Shipyard*

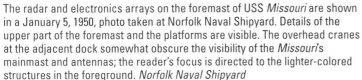

The radar and electronics arrays on the foremast of USS *Missouri* are shown in a January 5, 1950, photo taken at Norfolk Naval Shipyard. Details of the upper part of the foremast and the platforms are visible. The overhead cranes at the adjacent dock somewhat obscure the visibility of the *Missouri*'s mainmast and antennas; the reader's focus is directed to the lighter-colored structures in the foreground. *Norfolk Naval Shipyard*

Antennas and electronics on top of the mainmast of USS *Missouri* are seen close-up from an elevated position to the port side at Norfolk on January 5, 1950. The dark-colored antenna slightly above the center of the photo is the SG radar. The SP height-finder radar is the dish antenna to the lower right; note the mesh construction of the dish. *Norfolk Naval Shipyard*

CHAPTER 8
Aground

In stark contrast to the dignified manner in which the crew of *Missouri* presented the ship following the Japanese surrender, the events of January 17, 1950, were at the time very much an embarrassment for the Navy.

Capt. William D. Brown, skipper of the *Missouri* since December 10, 1949, and an experienced destroyerman but new to battleships, prepared to take the ship through an acoustical range off Old Point Comfort, near Norfolk, Virginia. This was done at the request of the Naval Ordnance Laboratory, which desired to record the sound of the ship in the water as part of a program to identify warships by their unique sounds. The ship's navigator was Lt. Cmdr. Frank Morris, who had come aboard in January as well, as had the assistant navigator, Ens. E. R. Harris. The executive officer was Cmdr. George Peckham, who had more time aboard *Missouri* than the others.

In an attempt to run the acoustic range, at 8:10 Capt. Brown ordered a course of 060 degrees. Strong currents caused this course to be altered to 058 degrees. As Cmdr. Peckham passed through the chart room, he noticed the course plot and immediately told navigator Morris, "For God's sake watch it!" Concurrently, at 8:12, Capt. Brown was ordering *Missouri*'s speed be brought up to 15 knots, believing this would provide better rudder response than at slower speeds. At about this time, Lt. Ed Arnold, officer of the deck, noticed a small orange-and-white buoy 1,000 yards away. Believing that this was the marker for the right side of the acoustic range, Capt. Brown ordered *Missouri* quartermaster Bevan Travis to turn to a course of 053, in order to pass to the left of the marker. Knowing this to be a problem, Travis questioned the captain twice, with the second eliciting a response of to do what he was told. The next buoys that were sighted marked the beginning of a small fishing channel, but *Missouri*'s skipper thought instead that they marked the end of the acoustic range.

Following a week of modernization and repair work at Norfolk Naval Shipyard in early January 1950, the *Missouri* was departing for a voyage to Guantánamo Bay, Cuba, on January 17, when she ran aground on Thimble Shoals, off Old Point Comfort, Virginia. This photo of the port side of the stern while the ship was grounded shows the extent to which the lower hull was exposed at low tide. Worthy of notice are the dimpling of the shell (the hull plates) from the stresses of service, the thirteen ladder rungs on the stern, the ship's name painted white, the mooring chocks, and the aft port quad 40 mm gun mount and its sponson. *Naval History and Heritage Command*

Four decks below, Cmdr. Peckham at 8:15 sent a message to Brown, saying, "Ship heading into danger shoals. Recommend you come right immediately!" Simultaneously, navigator Morris again recommended coming to the right. Getting no response, Morris then rushed toward the captain, waving his arms and shouting, "Come right, there's shoal water ahead!" Brown again dismissed this warning, responding by telling the operations officer, Cmdr. John Millett, "I don't believe the navigator knows

Tugs alongside the *Missouri* are straining to back her off Thimble Shoals, while a phalanx of tugs in the background pull on a tow hawser, during one of five attempts to unground the battleship between January 17 and February 1, 1950. *Naval History and Heritage Command*

A navy oiler is moored along the starboard side USS *Missouri* during her grounding on Thimble Shoals. The oiler was taking fuel off the battleship in an effort to reduce her draft, in the ongoing efforts to unground her.

Crewmen on the *Missouri* watch expectantly as a tugboat maneuvers in close to the battleship during an attempt to unground her. The view is abeam turret 3 on the port side of the ship.

The navy tried a number of extraordinary measures during the efforts to refloat the *Missouri* at Thimble Shoals in the last half of January 1950. Here, an explosive charge weighing 75 pounds has been detonated underwater off the starboard stern in an effort to prepare the way for refloating the ship. Two such charges were detonated on that day. *Norfolk Naval Shipyard*

The *Missouri* is viewed from above her bow, with eight tugboats attempting to unground her from Thimble Shoals. Faintly visible on the roof of turret 1 is the battleship's number, "63," painted in white and oriented with the tops of the numerals forward. *Naval History and Heritage Command*

USS *Missouri* is viewed off her bow during an attempt by tugboats to free her at Thimble Shoals. Minesweepers and other craft are in the channel in the background. Faintly visible on the forecastle are two twin 20 mm gun mounts. A large number of sailors dressed in whites are on the deck. *National Archives*

where we are; go find out." In a concession that his subordinates might be right, Capt. Brown ordered the modest course adjustment to 058 degrees. But by then it was too late: the bow of *Missouri* struck mud at 8:17 as quartermaster Bevan Travis swung the wheel as ordered by Brown. *Missouri*, making 12½ knots on the way to the 15 knots ordered by her captain, traveled almost a half mile with her belly on the mud flat, lifting the waterline of the behemoth 8 feet above the surface of Chesapeake Bay.

At 8:30 the call went out from *Missouri* for tugs to assist the battleship, now landlocked within sight of the headquarters of the Navy yard at Norfolk. Those initial efforts were unsuccessful, and soon enough the job was turned over to the commandant of

the navy yard, RAdm. Homer N. Wallin, who incidentally had overseen the salvage of the fleet at Pearl Harbor.

After removing the ammunition, fuel, food, and loose gear; dredging and attaching floatation pontoons; and awaiting for an unusually high tide, on February 1 *Missouri* was finally freed. She then went to the navy yard for repair, which was completed by February 7. With Capt. Page Smith again in command (Brown having been relieved following the grounding, and ultimately court-martialed), *Missouri* was ready to rejoin the fleet, with no lasting damage to the ship itself, only to the pride of the crew and the US Navy.

During one of the attempts to unground USS *Missouri*, a row of tugboats are pulling on one or more hawsers attached to the stern of the battleship, trying to pull the ship off Thimble Shoals. One tugboat is pushing against the row of tugs to keep them on course. In addition, other tugboats are alongside the *Missouri* to assist in the effort. *National Archives*

After being ungrounded on February 1, 1950, USS *Missouri* proceeded to the Portsmouth Navy Yard, where she is seen going into drydock. There, her hull would be inspected for damage from the grounding, and repairs would be made. The man to the right is using a microphone and hand signals to send instructions to the towline handlers who are on each side of the dock.

This final photo in the series documenting the grounding of the *Missouri* on Thimble Shoals was taken on January 20, 1950, and is a closer view of the operation shown in the preceding photo. The tug in the right foreground is pulling a hawser secured to the second tug from the left in the immediate background. It required dredging an escape channel, plus the assistance of the tugboats, to finally unground the *Missouri* on February 1, 1950.

Tugboats are assisting USS *Missouri* out of drydock at Portsmouth, Virginia, on February 8, 1950, following inspections and repairs after the ship's grounding. The next task for the ship was the testing of her engines before she put out for sea for a test run on the following day.

CHAPTER 9
Korea

After the *Missouri* received repairs in drydock at Portsmouth and her systems tested as satisfactory, she proceeded to Guantánamo Bay, Cuba, following which the battleship proceeded with Task Group 104.3 to participate in a series of war games designated Operation Carbex 50, in the Caribbean. Here, Marines are manning a battery of twin 20 mm guns, firing at radio-controlled target drones, during Carbex on March 15, 1950. *National Archives*

When North Korea invaded the south on June 25, 1950, *Missouri* was under the command of Capt. Irving Duke, who had relieved Capt. Smith in April. The ship had been officially relegated to a training role and had aboard a group of midshipmen, bound for Panama.

The mighty battleship would begin one more midshipman cruise that year, but that cruise was interrupted by the decision to send the *Missouri* where her big guns would do the most good—Korea. *Missouri* put into Norfolk, rather than the scheduled destination of Guantánamo. There, the midshipmen were offloaded for return to school, while for the next five days massive amounts of ammunition and provisions were loaded, and an additional thirty-six officers and 952 enlisted men came aboard, in order to bring her crew up to war footing, rather than the reduced crew needed to operate a training ship.

En route to Korea via the Panama Canal, *Missouri* passed through the outskirts of a hurricane, the high winds of which destroyed one whaleboat and caused others to become battering rams, pushing two HO3S helicopters over the side. The storm destroyed a 40 mm gun mount, which had to be replaced once the ship arrived at Pearl Harbor. While at Pearl, additional 20 mm guns, in the form of dual mounts, were installed.

On September 15, 1950, after steaming over 10,000 miles, *Missouri* arrived off the coast of Korea and immediately opened fire with her 16-inch rifles. With the fitting call sign "Battleax," *Missouri* rendered gunnery support for troops ashore. By the time the *Missouri*'s initial Korean deployment ended in March 1951, she had fired 2,895 16-inch rounds and 8,043 5-inch rounds at the enemy.

For much of the remainder of 1951, the ship resumed her training duties, as well as an overhaul, which was followed by more training and a cruise to Europe in company with her sister ship *Wisconsin*, which had been removed from the mothball fleet and reactivated in light of the Korean situation. By October *Missouri* was alongside elder sister and lead ship of the class *Iowa* at Yoksuka, Japan, before moving on to the Korean coast and a resumption of bombardment.

Shore bombardment continued into March 1953. As the ship began to make her way home, her skipper, Capt. Warner Edsall, died while on the bridge. After the ship's return stateside, she continued to be used for training service as well as the occasional "showing of the flag" overseas until early 1955, when, with Truman no longer in office to protect her, she was put out into Puget Sound Naval Shipyard and had her systems preserved, joining the naval reserve fleet there. On February 26, 1955, the *Missouri* was decommissioned.

When war broke out on the Korean Peninsula in the summer of 1950, USS *Missouri* returned to combat duty, sailing by way of the Panama Canal to the Pacific and arriving off the Korean coast on September 15. Two days later, on September 17, Cmdr. William H. Hoffman, chaplain, is conducting religious services on the fantail of the *Missouri*. In the background is a Sikorsky HU-1 helicopter, the bureau number of which appears to be 123125. *National Archives*

The forward part of USS *Missouri* is viewed from the pilothouse during operations in the Korean War. On the roof of turret 1 are the ship's number, "63," and a US flag, for aerial recognition. The ship was leaving the coast of Korea, bound for Japan, on September 17, 1950, after several days of shore bombardment. *National Archives*

Personnel are attentively executing their duties in one of USS *Missouri*'s two main-battery plotting rooms during operations off Korea on September 17, 1950. The plotting rooms were the centers where personnel received data from the main-battery directors and, in combination with analog computers and gyroscopes, formulated firing solutions for the ship's 116-inch/50-caliber guns. *National Archives*

The 16-inch/50-caliber guns of turret 1 of USS *Missouri* are trained to port in preparation for firing during the October 12, 1950, bombardment of Chongjin, on the eastern coast of Korea. The wooden parts of the deck are unpainted, while the metal surfaces on the edges of the deck, on the forecastle, and on the tops of the turrets are painted Deck Blue. *National Archives*

Turret two is firing a salvo of 16-inch shells during the bombardment of Chongjin, North Korea, on October 12, 1950. The bombardment was part of an effort to interdict enemy communications lines. This photo is from a black-and-white negative, with colorized blast. *National Archives*

In a view looking down from the port side of the superstructure of the *Missouri* off the Korean coast on November 28, 1950, high lines have been rigged from the battleship to the oiler USS *Cimarron* (AO-22) in order to transfer personnel to the oiler. The *Cimarron* had just finished refueling the *Missouri*. *National Archives*

Four days before Christmas 1950 off the Korean coast, three members of the USS *Missouri*'s crew are decorating a Christmas tree. They are, left to right, Marine Pfc. Charles A. McConnell and Seamen Edwin F. Pawlak (partially hidden behind the tree) and Enoch Smith. *National Archives*

During a nighttime bombardment in late December 1950, the right gun of turret 1 of USS *Missouri* has just fired a 16-inch shell at Communist forces attacking Hungnam, North Korea. In the background, landing ships, medium (LSMRs), are firing rockets at targets onshore, with both ends of the trajectory visible. This is a composite photograph, made by combining two negatives taken a few minutes apart. *Naval History and Heritage Command*

Smoke from the gun blast dissipates following the firing of the 16-inch/50-caliber guns of turret 3 during the bombardment of Communist forces at Kansong, North Korea, in February 1951. The view is from the starboard side of the forward fire-control tower. *National Archives*

In a photograph dated February 5, 1951, crewmen of USS *Missouri* are stacking empty 5-inch powder casings on a deck adjacent to a twin 5-inch/38-caliber gun mount during a shore bombardment. Visible to the upper right on the rear of the shield, or gunhouse, as the thinly armored enclosure of the 5-inch/38-caliber gun mount is called, are an open access door and case-ejector ports. *National Archives*

Turret 3 is trained to port during a shore bombardment in February 1951. In the background, the 16-inch/50-caliber guns of turrets 1 and 2 have just unleashed a broadside. High above turret 3 atop the aft fire-control tower, the aft Mk.38 main-battery director is trained to port so that its occupants can observe the target area. *National Archives*

A photographer on the bridge of the *Missouri* captured the moment the big guns of turrets 1 and 2 fired to starboard during a shore bombardment Kansong, Korea, on February 5, 1951. To the lower left, the starboard side of the roof of the conning tower is visible. *National Archives*

At a naval base in February 1951, crewmen are loading 16-inch projectiles onto shell carts aboard USS *Missouri* in preparation for renewed bombardment operations against Communist forces in Korea. The projectiles will be sent to magazines far below decks.
Naval History and Heritage Command

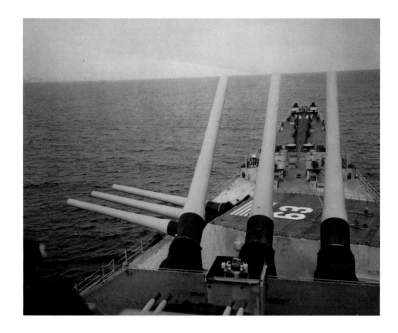

Turrets 1 and 2 of USS *Missouri* have paused firing momentarily during a shore bombardment off Kansong, Korea, on February 5, 1951. In the foreground, to the front of the barrels of the quad 40 mm gun mount on top of turret 2, is the Mk.51 director for that gun mount, inside a box-shaped, open-topped splinter shield. *Naval History and Heritage Command*

Five tugboats, four toward the bow and one farther aft, are assisting USS *Missouri* into her berth upon arriving at Norfolk, Virginia, on April 27, 1951. The ship had departed from the Far East in late March, ending her first deployment to Korea. *National Archives*

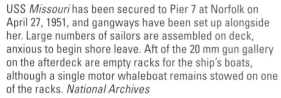

USS *Missouri* has been secured to Pier 7 at Norfolk on April 27, 1951, and gangways have been set up alongside her. Large numbers of sailors are assembled on deck, anxious to begin shore leave. Aft of the 20 mm gun gallery on the afterdeck are empty racks for the ship's boats, although a single motor whaleboat remains stowed on one of the racks. *National Archives*

The *Missouri* is seen from the opposite angle depicted in the preceding photo, docked at Pier 7 at Norfolk on April 27, 1951. The US flag and the number "63," seen on the roof of turret 1 in photos of the ship at war in Korea, had been painted over. Moored on the other side of the dock are USS *Albany* (CA-123), and USS *Macon* (CA-132). *National Archives*

In the late spring and summer of 1951, USS *Missouri* hosted another midshipmen's cruise. This June 5 photo shows a gunner's mate instructing midshipmen in the operation of the quad 40 mm antiaircraft guns on top of turret 2. To the front of the gun mount on the turret roof is the Mk.51 director associated with that mount. It is rare to see the splinter shield with its four sides, hinged at the bottom, in the folded-down position, allowing a view of the director and its pedestal. *National Archives*

From the fall of 1951 to January 1952, USS *Missouri* had her first major repairs and modernization since the winter of 1949–50. The work was done at the Norfolk Naval Shipyard. The forward part of the ship is seen from above on or around January 19, 1952, near the end of that period of modernization. Turret 1, to the extreme right, is traversed to port. *Norfolk Naval Shipyard*

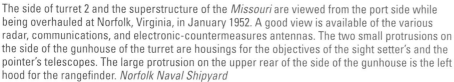

The side of turret 2 and the superstructure of the *Missouri* are viewed from the port side while being overhauled at Norfolk, Virginia, in January 1952. A good view is available of the various radar, communications, and electronic-countermeasures antennas. The two small protrusions on the side of the gunhouse of the turret are housings for the objectives of the sight setter's and the pointer's telescopes. The large protrusion on the upper rear of the side of the gunhouse is the left hood for the rangefinder. *Norfolk Naval Shipyard*

The forward part of the *Missouri* is viewed from above her port beam during an inclining experiment near the conclusion of her modernization work in the Norfolk Naval Shipyard on January 19, 1952. An inclining experiment is performed on a ship once it has been completed, or when major structural changes have been done to her. It involves placing heavy weights on various parts of the decks and then moving the weights while using instruments called stabilographs to record the ship's deflections. All of this was done to establish the metacentric height of the ship, which is necessary to know to ensure the stability and proper loading of the ship. *Norfolk Naval Shipyard*

A view of the *Missouri* from a pier at Norfolk includes details of turret 2 and the superstructure. Just above and aft of the top of the forward secondary-battery director, midway up the forward fire-control tower, is an open bridge. This fronted on the primary conning station or wheel house, inside the fire-control tower, from which the movements of the ship were controlled during noncombat operations. *Norfolk Naval Shipyard*

The primary conning station and its open bridge are seen to good advantage in this photo taken during *Missouri*'s inclining experiment. The conning station has a curved front, with round portholes. Higher up on the forward fire-control tower is the forward air-defense station, an open platform where sky lookouts and target designators were stationed. Above the forward air-defense station is the forward Mk.38 main-battery director, showing the supports for the Mk.13 radar antenna on the roof of the director. *Norfolk Naval Shipyard*

Another photo taken during the inclining experiment on January 19, 1952, focuses on the aft part of the superstructure. To the rear of the aft smokestack is the conical-shaped rear fire-control tower, on top of which is the aft Mk.38 main-battery director, with a Mk.13 radar antenna on top of it. To the rear of the aft fire-control tower is the aft Mk.37 secondary-battery director, with a dish-type Mk.25 radar antenna on top of it. *Norfolk Naval Shipyard*

In a close view of the rear of the superstructure and turret 3, between those two structures is a track to support and allow the cross-deck movement of heavy weights being used in the inclining experiment on January 19, 1952. The weights are visible on the starboard side of the track. A clear view is offered of the quad 40 mm gun mount on turret 3. Racks for 40 mm ammunition are visible on the interior of the splinter shield for the mount. On the rear of the turret are two floater racks, containing nets that would float free should the ship be sunk, providing something for survivors to cling to. *Norfolk Naval Shipyard*

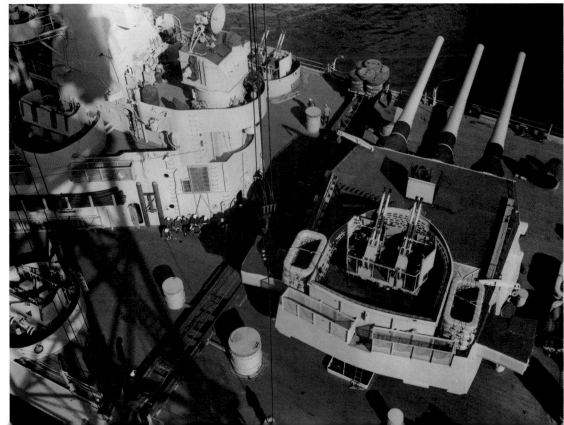

The aft part of USS *Missouri* is viewed from the starboard side during the inclining experiment at Norfolk. The box-shaped deck house aft of turret 3 was used as a movie projection booth. In the background is the aircraft carrier USS *Coral Sea* (CV-43). *Norfolk Naval Shipyard*

This final photo from the series taken during the *Missouri*'s January 19, 1952, inclining experiment captures the starboard side of the ship from the aft smokestack forward. The track used for holding and shuttling the forward set of weights in the inclining experiment is faintly visible on the main deck just aft of turret 1. After the completion of the overhaul, the *Missouri* would proceed to Cuban waters for military exercises. *Norfolk Naval Shipyard*

Following several training cruises in the Caribbean and the North Atlantic in the spring and summer of 1952, USS *Missouri* was redeployed to Korea. The *Missouri*, left, and her sister ship USS *Iowa*, right, are moored together at Yokosuka, Japan, sometime between October 18 and 20, 1952, at the time when the *Missouri* was relieving the *Iowa* as flagship of the Seventh Fleet. VAdm. Joseph J. Clark, commander of the Seventh Fleet, transferred his flag to the *Missouri* on October 19. Note the new-style large, white number "61" with black shadowing on the bow of the *Iowa*, while *Missouri* still has the old-type small number. *National Museum of Naval Aviation*

Sister ships USS *Iowa* (BB-61, left) and USS *Missouri* lie at anchor, side by side, at Yokosuka, Japan, in October 1952. This was during the transfer of the flag of Adm. Joseph "Jocko" Clark from the Iowa to the *Missouri*. Note the various boats stored on the fantails of the ships and the large stacks of ammunition on the deck of the Iowa. *National Museum of Naval Aviation*

During an overhaul of USS *Missouri* at Norfolk Naval Shipyard in January 1954, new barrels were installed on the 16-inch/50-caliber guns. In this photo, the center gun of turret 3 is being removed. Farther forward, scaffolding encloses the mainmast, which was being rebuilt from a tripod structure to one with four legs, to better support a new SPS-8 radar antenna.

Not only were the *Missouri*'s big 16-inch/50-caliber guns used in bombardments of targets onshore, the ship's 5-inch/38-caliber guns also were employed in these barrages. Here, spent propellant casings litter the deck behind one of *Missouri*'s twin 5-inch/38-caliber gun mounts during the bombardment of Wonsan, North Korea, on March 9, 1953. Note the blast hood and the ring sight for the mount captain atop the gunhouse. *National Archives*

Capt. Warner E. Edsall, commanding officer of USS *Missouri*, poses for his portrait to the front of turret 1 at Yokosuka, Japan, on January 14, 1953. Edsall assumed command of the *Missouri* on September 4, 1952, and served in that capacity until his unexpected death on March 26, 1953. *National Archives*

On March 26, 1953, Capt. Warner Edsall, the *Missouri*'s commanding officer, died suddenly of a heart attack while the battleship was maneuvering into the narrow confines of Sasebo Harbor in Japan. The ship's crew and visiting VIPs turned out on *Missouri*'s afterdeck for Edsall's memorial service at Sasebo. *National Archives*

All four battleships of the *Iowa* class were photographed together at sea on only one occasion, while serving with Battleship Division Two in the Virginia Capes operating area on June 7, 1954. The ships are, from foreground to background, USS *Iowa* (BB-61), USS *Wisconsin* (BB-64), USS *Missouri* (BB-63), and USS *New Jersey* (BB-62). *National Archives*

In another aerial photograph of Battleship Division Two on June 7, 1954, the ships are steaming in column, with USS *Wisconsin* leading. It is not certain which ship USS *Missouri* is. *National Archives*

In 1954, as a cost-cutting measure, the navy decided to inactivate USS *Missouri*. During that year, the size of the crew was drawn down as crewmen were reassigned to other ships or duties. In September 1954 the *Missouri* arrived at the Puget Sound Naval Shipyard, Bremerton, Washington, where the battleship was decommissioned on February 26, 1955. Here, Seaman Carl Dewesse, assisted by Fire Controlman Apprentice Lynn Jex, is lowering the ship's ensign on the stern during the decommissioning ceremony. *National Archives*

Following decommissioning, USS *Missouri* was placed in "mothballs," or long-term storage, at Puget Sound Naval Shipyard, as seen in this February 1955 photograph. Dome-shaped "igloos" or "cocoons" cover the quad 40 mm gun mounts. The blast bags have been removed from the 16-inch guns, and solid panels have been installed to fill the gaps between the gun barrels and the fronts of the gunhouses. Other measures had been taken to weatherproof, dehumidify, and seal the ship. *National Archives*

CHAPTER 10
Final Service

Sister ships USS *New Jersey* (BB-62), left, and USS *Missouri* (BB-63) are docked on either side of a naval inactive-ship maintenance facility pier at Puget Sound Naval Shipyard on July 1, 1981. During the *Missouri*'s long-term storage, visitors were allowed to tour limited areas of the ship. *US Navy*

Missouri, like her *Iowa*-class sisters *New Jersey*, *Wisconsin*, and *Iowa*, lingered for decades in the reserve fleet, since all the other battleships, not just in the US fleet but worldwide, were either converted to museums, in the case of a fortunate few, or, as in the case of most, reduced to scrap. The brief, but very effective, reactivation of the *New Jersey* during the Vietnam War proved the effectiveness of big guns, especially when, unlike aerial support, they can remain on station indefinitely.

Thus, in a decision that came as a surprise to some and a blessing to others (notably the Marines, who had long fought for the retention of the battleships), in the 1980s the Reagan administration's Secretary of the Navy John Lehman ordered the reactivation and modernization of the four *Iowas*.

Missouri was towed from Puget Sound to Long Beach in 1984 for refitting, work that was completed in 1986. The numerous 40 mm guns aboard the ship were removed, as were four of the ten 5-inch gun mounts. In their place were installed four Mk.141 quad cell launchers for sixteen RGM-84 Harpoon antiship missiles, eight armored box launcher (ABL) mounts for thirty-two BGM-109 Tomahawk missiles, and, replacing the bevy of 20 mm and 40 mm antiaircraft weapons of yesteryear, a quartet of 3,000 round-per-minute Phalanx close-in weapons system (CIWS) Gatling guns. While the profile of the ship was forever altered, unchanged was her heavy armor protection as well as the still-formidable main battery of nine 16-inch rifles.

Fittingly, one of the many dignitaries speaking at *Missouri*'s May 10, 1986, recommissioning was Margaret Truman Daniels, the ship's original sponsor, who admonished the crew and Capt. Albert Kaiss to "take care of my baby."

Missouri left Long Beach on September 10, 1986, on an around-the-world shakedown cruise, which concluded on December 19. For the next few years, *Missouri* was frequently called on to "show the flag," as well as going into harm's way in 1987 as part of Operation Earnest Will, escorting tankers in the Persian Gulf.

In 1989, *Missouri* made a somewhat unorthodox media appearance as the location for the music video of Cher's "If I Could Turn Back Time" recording. This event, while very popular with the crew, was not well-received by the Navy, which had granted permission for this use.

On November 13, 1990, however, *Missouri* left her home port to take part in her final combat mission, taking part in the Gulf War to drive Saddam Hussein's Iraqi forces out of Kuwait. In the opening hours of Operation Desert Storm, *Missouri* fired her first Tomahawk cruise missile at 1:40 a.m. on January 17, 1991. Over the next five days, a further twenty-seven such missiles were fired. On January 29, her big guns joined the action, shelling Iraqi command installations. By February 26, the ground war had moved out of range of *Missouri*, and after a brief period enforcing an armistice, she turned toward home. During the Gulf War she had fired 783 16-inch rounds and twenty-eight Tomahawks.

In early 1984, the Navy made preparations to send the battleship *Missouri* to the Long Beach Naval Shipyard in California for modernization and reactivation. The ship is seen here on May 14, 1984, as it begins its voyage from Bremerton, Washington, to Long Beach. Behind the *Missouri*, a fireboat sends up streams of water to celebrate the battleship's next phase. *Puget Sound Naval Shipyard*

The forward part of the battleship *Missouri* is viewed from high up in the superstructure while undergoing modernization at the Long Beach Naval Shipyard in California in or around June 1984. The protective igloos are still on the 40 mm gun mounts. *US Navy*

Despite this effective use, the decision was reached to again retire the battleships. Though her sisters were decommissioned in short order, *Missouri* was kept in commission long enough to be present during the fiftieth-anniversary ceremonies of the attack on Pearl Harbor. While at Pearl for this ceremony, the battleship hosted President George H. W. Bush. This event would be central to the script of *Missouri's* big-screen appearance in the 1992 film *Under Siege*, although the movie was actually filmed primarily aboard USS *Alabama*.

On March 31, 1992, at Puget Sound, *Missouri* was decommissioned yet again. Her captain at the time was again Albert L. Kaiss (although there had been two others since her recommissioning). Kaiss was the final man to leave the ship that day, making him the last battleship sailor.

Missouri remained part of the Reserve Fleet until January 12, 1995, when she was struck from the Naval Vessel Register. On May 4, 1998, custody of the ship was transferred to the USS *Missouri* Memorial Association, Honolulu, Hawaii. The battleship was towed to Pearl Harbor and moored at Ford Island, facing USS *Arizona*. She opened as a museum and monument on January 26, 1999.

The *Missouri* is undergoing work in drydock at Long Beach around mid-1984. The anchors have been removed, as have the quad 40 mm guns, including on the roof of turret 2. Scaffolding has been erected around the superstructure and forward smokestack, and an impressive new structure, the electronic countermeasures (ECM) compartment, has been constructed toward the top of the forward fire-control tower. For now, the Mk.38 secondary-battery director has been removed from the top of that tower. *US Navy*

In a rear view of the *Missouri* in drydock at Long Beach, the 40 mm gun mounts have been removed from the fantail, but the sponsons that supported the mounts remain in place. In the future, the sponsons would be used as stations for servicing helicopters. *US Navy*

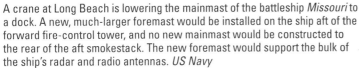

A crane at Long Beach is lowering the mainmast of the battleship *Missouri* to a dock. A new, much-larger foremast would be installed on the ship aft of the forward fire-control tower, and no new mainmast would be constructed to the rear of the aft smokestack. The new foremast would support the bulk of the ship's radar and radio antennas. *US Navy*

The front of the superstructure of the *Missouri* is encased in scaffolding as shipyard workers at Long Beach, California, modernize the battleship in preparation for its reactivation and recommissioning. To the rear and in line with the Mk.25 radar antenna on the forward Mk.37 director is the primary conning station, with its round portholes. Directly above the portholes are part of the support structure for the ECM compartment, which will later take shape around the upper part of the forward fire-control tower. *US Navy*

On May 6, 1986, newly modernized and ready to reenter active service in the navy, the battleship *Missouri* has arrived at San Francisco, California, where she will be recommissioned. Large harbor tugs are maneuvering her toward the dock where she will be recommissioned four days later. The Oakland Bay Bridge is in the background. Prominent on the forecastle is the newly installed antenna array for the Naval Tactical Data System (NTDS), part of an automated system for coordinating information on enemy targets. *US Navy*

Crewmen march double-time toward the gangways at the *Missouri*'s recommissioning ceremony. Some of the new features in view include two whip antennas at the front of the pilothouse, the ECM compartment, the foremast and its antennas, a boat davit aft of the second twin 5-inch/38-caliber gun mount, and the outrigger for the underway replenishment (UNREP) system, aft of the rear 5-inch mount. *US Navy*

Margaret Truman Daniels, the daughter of President Harry S. Truman, and the sponsor who christened the battleship *Missouri* in January 1944, addresses those convened for the recommissioning of the ship on May 10, 1986. *US Navy*

Crewmen board the *Missouri* during her recommissioning ceremony. Above and slightly to the right of the Marine guard in the foreground, on a platform decorated with bunting, is one of the new Phalanx Mk.15 close-in weapons system (CIWS) mounts. These self-contained systems, of which four were installed, feature a 20 mm M61 Vulcan gun along with K-band radar and fire-control systems. They were designed to combat aircraft and antiship missiles. *US Navy*

A CH-53E Super Stallion from Helicopter Combat Support Squadron 4 (CH-4) carrying Italian news reporters is about to touch down on the helipad of USS *Missouri* in November 1986. The ship was about to visit Naples, Italy, during an around-the-world shakedown cruise. *US Navy*

Visitors on the foredeck of USS *Missouri* on a Dependents' Day cruise in 1989 cover their ears as the 16-inch/50-caliber guns let loose with a broadside during a firepower demonstration. Some, but not all, of the spectators are wearing ear protectors. *US Navy*

As photographed from an aircraft during 1987, USS *Missouri* has just fired a broadside to starboard from its 16-inch/50-caliber guns during a main-battery firing exercise. Worthy of notice are the number "63" on the roof of turret 1, the white markings on the helipad on the fantail, and the light-colored Mk.143 armored box launchers (ABLs) for the BGM-109 Tomahawk cruise missiles arranged around the aft smokestack. Installed during the 1984—86 modernization of the *Missouri*, the Tomahawks gave the ship the ability to reach out to well over 1,000 miles with highly accurate cruise missiles armed with conventional or nuclear warheads. *US Navy*

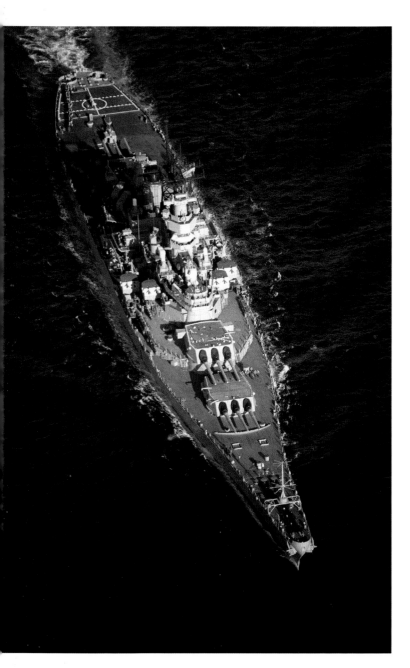

The 20 mm Vulcan gun of a Mark 15 Phalanx close-in weapons system (CIWS) is firing during gunnery practice on USS *Missouri* during 1989. The shape of the white equipment pod and radome on top of the mount lent the CIWS the nickname "R2D2." *US Navy*

USS *Missouri* is at sea during 1989. The ship was painted overall in Haze Gray, with wooden parts of the decks not painted. Metal decks, the helipad, and the turret tops had a dark-gray nonskid finish. *US Navy*

A 1989 photograph of two Mk.143 ABLs for Tomahawk cruise missiles aboard *Missouri* shows one in the raised position for firing and the other in the stored position. The ship had eight ABLs, each of which carried four canister-mounted BGM-109 Tomahawk antiship missiles (TASMs) and Tomahawk land attack missiles (TLAMs). Launching canisters are not installed in these ABLs. *US Navy*

A BGM-109 Tomahawk missile launch is viewed from the port side of the *Missouri*'s foredeck during the early part of Operation Desert Storm. By January 20, 1991, the ship had launched a total of twenty-one Tomahawks at Iraqi ground forces. *US Navy*

A BGM-109 TLAM has just been fired from an ABL on USS *Missouri* during the early part of Operation Desert Storm, the combat phase of the 1990–91 Gulf War. The missile was directed at an Iraqi target. The *Missouri* first fired its Tomahawk missiles in anger in the early hours of January 17, 1991. *US Navy*

During Operation Desert Storm, USS *Missouri*'s primary and secondary gun batteries were employed against Iraqi forces. Here, 16-inch/50-caliber guns of turret 1 are firing during the night at an Iraqi target along the northern coast of Kuwait. The guns of turret 2 are elevated to the starboard for firing, as are the 5-inch/38-caliber guns in the foreground. *US Navy*

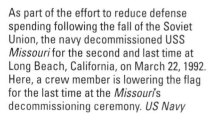

As part of the effort to reduce defense spending following the fall of the Soviet Union, the navy decommissioned USS *Missouri* for the second and last time at Long Beach, California, on March 22, 1992. Here, a crew member is lowering the flag for the last time at the *Missouri*'s decommissioning ceremony. *US Navy*

Members of the crew of the *Missouri* disembark from the ship for the last time at the conclusion of the decommissioning ceremony at Long Beach on March 22, 1992. *US Navy*

Secretary of the Navy John H. Dalton signs the agreement by which the battleship *Missouri* will be sent to Pearl Harbor, Hawaii, for use as a museum ship. The signing took place in Washington, DC, on May 4, 1998. The *Missouri* was to be docked near the battleship *Arizona* (BB-39) Memorial. *US Navy*

The battleship *Missouri* was towed from Bremerton, Washington, where she had been stored for several years, 2,600 miles across the Pacific to her new home at Pearl Harbor in June 1998. Here, the ship is being maneuvered into her new berth at Fox 5 S-N alongside Ford Island (right) and adjacent to the USS *Arizona* memorial (foreground). *US Navy*

On January 7, 2010, the battleship *Missouri* is departing the Pearl Harbor Naval Shipyard's Dry Dock 4 following a three-month period of preservation and maintenance work that cost $8 million. The ship was bound for her pier next to Ford Island. *US Navy*

From the pier of the Battleship *Missouri* Memorial, visitors also may enjoy this view of the aft part of the starboard side of the aft part of the superstructure. To the front of the aft smokestack is the port boat davit with a boat stored below it. Adjacent to the aft smokestack and above the twin 5-inch/38-caliber gun mount are launchers for Harpoon antiship missiles, which were installed during the 1980s modernization of the ship. Farther aft, alongside the aft fire-control tower, a Tomahawk cruise missile is displayed. On the pier in the foreground is a quad 40 mm antiaircraft gun mount of the type used on the ship during World War II and the Korean War. *Tom Kailbourn*

For visitors approaching the Battleship *Missouri* Memorial at Pearl Harbor, this is one of the first views that greets them: the port side of the forward part of the superstructure, as photographed in October 2011. Aft of the pilothouse is the ship's scoreboard, decorated with her campaign ribbons and efficiency awards. Above the scoreboard is the forward Mk.37 director and one of the Phalanx Mk.15 close-in weapons system mounts. Also in view are two of the twin 5-inch/38-caliber dual-purpose gun mounts. *Tom Kailbourn*

The tops of turrets 1 and 2 are viewed from the open bridge to the front of the top level of the conning tower, one level above the pilothouse on the *Missouri*, in October 2011. The roof of turret 2 is covered with a rubber-based nonskid surface. Mounted on it are a collapsible tripod, employed in high-line transfer operations while at sea, as well as a number of white-painted pad eyes. In the background, to the front of the *Missouri*, is the *Arizona* Memorial. *Tom Kailbourn*

One of the iconic battleships of all history, the battleship *Missouri* fought in three wars and was the scene of one of the key events of the twentieth century: the signing of the Japanese surrender document at the conclusion of World War II. The *Missouri* survives as a museum ship, where visitors can absorb her rich history and pay tribute to the courageous men and women who served on her. Here, USS *Missouri* is viewed from her aft starboard quarter in her berth at Pearl Harbor on June 20, 2016, with the USS *Arizona* memorial to her front. These two battleship memorials are rich in symbolism: one, the *Arizona*, marks the entrance of the United States into World War II, and the other, the *Missouri*, represents the Allies' ultimate victory in that war. *US Navy*